PRESENTING
Cynthia Voigt

Twayne's United States Authors Series
Young Adult Authors

Patricia J. Campbell, General Editor

TUSAS 643

PRESENTING

Cynthia Voigt

Suzanne Elizabeth Reid

Twayne Publishers
An Imprint of Simon & Shuster Macmillan
New York

Prentice Hall International
London Mexico City New Delhi Singapore Sydney Toronto

Chapter 3 first appeared in briefer form as "Images in Cynthia Voigt's Tillerman Series," *The ALAN Review*, fall 1991, pp. 10–14. Reprinted by permission.

Part of chapter 4 first appeared in "Feminist Issues in Cynthia Voigt's *Jackaroo, Seventeen Against the Dealer*, and *On Fortune's Wheel*," published in the fall 1992 issue of the *SIGNAL Journal*. Reprinted with permission.

The four lines from "The Frog Prince" by Stevie Smith quoted in chapter 6 first appeared in *The Frog Prince and Other Poems* by Stevie Smith (New York: McKay, 1966), p. 88. Reprinted by permission.

All the photographs herein are by Walter Voigt and are published with the kind permission of Cynthia Voigt.

Twayne's United States Authors Series No. 643

Presenting Cynthia Voigt
Suzanne Elizabeth Reid

Twayne Publishers
An Imprint of Simon & Schuster Macmillan
866 Third Avenue
New York, NY 10022

Library of Congress Cataloging-in-Publication Data

Reid, Suzanne Elizabeth.
    Presenting Cynthia Voigt / Suzanne Elizabeth Reid.
       p. cm. — (Twayne's United States authors series : TUSAS 643)
    Based on the author's thesis (Ph. D.)—Virginia Polytechnic Institute and State University.
    Includes bibliographical references and index.
    ISBN 0-8057-8219-2
    1. Voigt, Cynthia—Criticism and interpretation. 2. Young adult fiction, American—History and criticism. [1. Voight, Cynthia.
2. American literature—History and criticism.] I. Title.
II. Series.
PS3572.O33Z85   1995
813'.54—dc20
                                94-44197
                                    CIP
                                    AC

*In memory of my mother, Marjorie Bradlee Schmid,
and my uncles, Paul and John Schmid,
who lived as fully as any of Cynthia Voigt's heroes*

Contents

Foreword

The advent of Twayne's Young Adult Author Series in 1985 was a response to the growing stature and value of adolescent literature and the lack of serious critical evaluation of the new genre. The first volume of the series was heralded as marking the coming-of-age of young adult fiction.

The aim of the series is twofold. First, it enables young readers to research the work of their favorite authors, and to see them as real people. Each volume is written in a lively, readable style and attempts to present in an attractive, accessible format a vivid portrait of the author as a person.

Second, the series provides teachers and librarians with insights and background material for promoting and teaching young adult novels. Each of the biocritical studies is a serious literary analysis of one author's work (or one subgenre within young adult literature), with attention to plot structure, theme, character, setting, and imagery. In addition, many of the series writers delve deeper into the creative writing process by tracking down early drafts or unpublished manuscripts by their subject authors, consulting with their editors or other mentors, and examining influences from literature, film, or social movements.

Many of the contributing authors of the series are among the leading scholars and critics of adolescent literature. Some are even young adult novelists themselves. Most of the studies are based on extensive interviews with the subject author, and each includes an exhaustive study of his or her work. Although the general format is the same, the individual volumes are uniquely shaped by their subjects, and each brings a different perspective to the classroom.

The goal of the series is to produce a succinct but comprehensive study of the life and art of every leading young adult author writing in the United States today. The books trace how that art has been accepted by readers and critics, evaluate its place in the developing field of adolescent literature, and—perhaps most important—inspire a reading and rereading of this quality fiction that speaks so directly to young people about their life's experience.

PATRICIA J. CAMPBELL, General Editor

Preface

I discovered Cynthia Voigt's works by accident. Browsing in a library, I came across *Homecoming*, read the first page and, like thousands of other readers, began to care, first, about the Tillermans, and then about Gwyn, Birle, Henry, Jean, Izzy, Gregor, Orien, and Oriel. These characters are not all people that you or I might like, but Voigt lets you know enough about them to get you to care. They come to life in your mind with all their questions and decisions, their problems and their solutions. Like close friends who let you know all that they are thinking, Voigt's characters explain alternate ways of meeting life.

As a teacher, I value Cynthia Voigt's works because they realistically depict the dilemmas of young adults as they dare to experiment with ways to define themselves. Her conversational style shows a respect for the way young people think and communicate with each other. As a woman, I appreciate how Voigt grapples with the issue of gender-defined roles in a nonsexist manner. She defies conventional assumptions about the roles of both males and females, letting her characters develop into people who are more than stereotypes. As an individual, I respect Voigt's work because she creates people who strive to learn and to define an individual self, but who also finally recognize the importance of maintaining and nurturing a connection to family and friends. I believe that the cycle of questioning, learning, and reaffirming that Voigt models in her books creates vital individuals who form a healthy society. Her characters are problem-solvers who actively care about themselves and the world in which they live, and these are the kind of people I want my students to know.

I want to acknowledge the editorial assistance of my husband, whose scholarly interest in Shakespeare's vision of life inspired him to ask hard questions about the thematic patterns of Voigt's work; he insisted that I respect her work enough to compare the two and that I respect myself enough to revise, rewrite, and revise again. I am deeply indebted to my professors at Virginia Tech, who encouraged me to write the dissertation on which this work is based: Dr. Pat Kelly, Dr. Robert Small, and Dr. Jim Garrison all asked important questions and provided much personal support. Dr. Kay Vandergrift kindly provided me with tapes of her delightful interview with Cynthia Voigt and with the photographs in this book. I appreciate both her knowledge of young adult literature, which inspired her insightful questions, and her generosity in lending me her tapes of the interview.

Especially, I want to thank Patricia J. Campbell, the general editor of Twayne's United States Authors Series: Young Adult Authors, who provided me this opportunity to write and assisted me in accomplishing this analysis of Voigt's work. I hope it proves even half as thought-provoking as the novels themselves.

Chronology

1942 Cynthia Irving born 25 February in Boston, Massachusetts.

Decides she wants to become a writer in ninth grade.

Graduates from the Dana Hill School.

1963 Graduates from Smith College with a B.A.

1964 Works as secretary for the J. Walter Thompson Advertising Agency in New York.

Marries Donald A. Booth and moves to New Mexico.

1965–1967 Teaches English at The Key School in Annapolis, Maryland.

1968–1969 Appointed English Department chair.

1971 Daughter Jessica born.

Divorces Donald Booth.

1971–1979 Continues as part-time teacher and department chair.

1974 Marries Walter Voigt, a teacher of Latin and Greek at The Key School.

1975–1976 Writes first draft of *The Callender Papers*.

1977 Son Peter (nicknamed Duffle) born.

1978 Writes *Tell Me If the Lovers Are Losers*.

1979 Writes *Homecoming.*

1981 *Homecoming* published; selected as a Notable Children's Trade Book in the Field of Social Studies. Nominated for an American Book Award.

1982 *Tell Me If the Lovers Are Losers* published; elected as an American Library Association Best Book for Young Adults.

Dicey's Song is published.

1983 Receives Newbery Medal for *Dicey's Song*; selected an American Library Association Best Children's Book.

A Solitary Blue (Newbery Honor Book and ALA Best Book for Young Adults).

The Callender Papers (The Edgar Allan Poe Award).

1984 *Building Blocks.*

1985 *The Runner.*

Jackaroo.

1986 *Izzy, Willy-Nilly.*

Come a Stranger.

Stories About Rosie, illustrated by Dennis Kendrick.

1987 *Sons from Afar.*

1988 *Tree by Leaf.*

1989 *Seventeen Against the Dealer.*

Receives the ALAN Award (Assembly on Literature for Adolescents), given by the National Council of Teachers of English for significant contribution to the field of adolescent literature.

1990 *On Fortune's Wheel* named by the American Library Association as a Best Book for Young Adults.

1991 *The Vandemark Mummy* and *Glass Mountain*.

1992 *David and Jonathan* and *Orfe*.

1993 *The Wings of a Falcon*.

1994 *When She Hollers*.

1. Cynthia Voigt: Adventurer Beneath the Surface

"I actually remember very little of my childhood, which makes me think it was quite happy. I suspect it might have been very close to perfect,"[1] writes Cynthia Voigt of her early life, which friends have characterized as normal and dull. Maybe on the outside: "Inside, secretly, invisibly, the right writing of a paragraph or a good telling of a story tastes like an adventure as exciting as any I've heard about, taken part in, or imagined."[2]

Becoming A Writer

Born in Boston, Massachusetts, on 25 February 1942 to Frederick C. Irving, a corporate executive, and Elise Keeney Irving, Cynthia is part of a family that includes an older sister, a younger sister, and twin brothers thirteen years younger than she. Cynthia does remember that she lived in rural southern Connecticut in houses with spacious yards. She started nursery school early, supposedly to bolster her shy older sister. "When it came time for the nursery school play, however, she was Miss Muffet, and I was the Spider. Later, when we got to dancing school—she was a Sweet Pea, and I was a Head of Cabbage" (Commire, 221).

Cynthia found young adult literature at her grandmother's house in northern Connecticut, with its shelves and shelves of books. There she became acquainted with *The Black Stallion* and

Cynthia Voigt as a child. "Is this me or my sister? We looked alike as children."

the Nancy Drew and Cherry Ames series. Frances Hodgson Burnett's *The Secret Garden* was a particular favorite. At that time there were few books written specifically for young adults. Cynthia, like other good readers of her age, began to read those adult books deemed suitable for adolescents. In her case these included Tolstoy, Camus, and Shakespeare.

Cynthia followed the paths of her mother and father by attending a private boarding school, Dana Hill School in Wellesley, Massachusetts. There she experienced a great deal of intellectual as well as physical freedom. "We could go downtown on our own, which in the fifties in a girls' boarding school was just this side of licentious" (Commire, 221). In retrospect, Voigt feels that the school's trust encouraged the students to make responsible judgments on their own.

Although Cynthia decided to become a writer in the ninth grade and wrote some short stories and poems in her high school and college years, nothing she submitted was published. Perhaps this was because she sent manuscripts to only one publisher before giving up. "What I didn't realize was that you send things to more than one place. I figured that if they were good enough, then everybody would know it; and if somebody said no, that meant they weren't good enough."[3]

At Smith College in Northampton, Massachusetts, Cynthia took creative writing courses, but she does not think she learned much from them. After her graduation from Smith in 1963, she worked for a year in public relations for the J. Walter Thompson Advertising Agency in New York City. Her boss was a wonderful woman who was writing a centennial history and had performed in vaudeville, where she tap-danced while playing the xylophone blindfolded. Voigt's neighbors in the tiny Greenwich Village apartment she rented were also unusual characters: "The lady next door owned killer German Shepherds and was in the habit of talking to herself and answering herself while her dogs leapt savagely against her windows. It was a fun year" (Commire, 222).

In 1964, Voigt married Donald Booth and moved to Santa Fe, New Mexico, where, unable to find other work, she spent six months at a Christian Brothers college becoming accredited to teach. Like many other well-educated women of her era, Voigt had vowed never to find herself in front of a class. The minute she walked into the classroom, however, she knew she had found her niche. From 1965 to 1967, she taught in a public high school in Glen Burnie, Maryland. Three years later, she joined the faculty at The Key School in Annapolis, where she became department chair in 1969.

During most of her first marriage, which ended amicably with a divorce in 1971, Voigt did not write much. She thinks that perhaps her writer's block was a symptom of her unhappiness. Soon after her separation, however, she began to compose again. Living alone with her small daughter, she tutored during the day and wrote for at least an hour each evening. However, her stories from this period are either lost or hidden in the bottom of a box.

Discovering Young Adult Literature

At The Key School, Voigt was assigned to teach English at the second-, fifth-, and seventh-grade levels. In preparing for her classes, she discovered that good literature for young adults and juveniles "had the shape of real books—novels—for kids the age of my students" (Commire, 222). These inspired her to think about this audience for her own writing. Two books—recommended by her future mother-in-law, who was studying children's literature at the time—particularly impressed her: Louise Fitzhugh's *Harriet the Spy* and Julia Cunningham's *Dorp Dead*. Other favorites include Robert O'Brien's *Mrs. Frisbee and the Rats of NIMH*, Lloyd Alexander's *The Book of Three*, and short stories by Elaine Konigsburg.

In 1974 she married Walter Voigt, a teacher of Latin and Greek at The Key School. It was only after she became pregnant with their son Peter (nicknamed Duffle) in 1977 that she reduced her teaching load and began to write for more than an hour a day. Inspired by the Gothic novels she had read, Voigt wrote *The Callender Papers* as an exercise in plotting, which she felt was a weakness in her writing. She did not submit it for publication until several years later, when her daughter Jessica, bored, picked it up and read it "standing up—just as she read her beloved *Nancy Drew* books. 'Gee, I guess *The Callender Papers* works,'" thought Voigt (Commire, 224). After she polished the language and revised the dialogue to differentiate the characters, the book was published by Atheneum in 1983.

Walter Voigt is a man of many talents and interests. A teacher, he also plays several musical instruments, reads widely, plays soccer, and is a photographer.

When her son was a year old, Voigt wrote the first draft of *Tell Me If the Lovers Are Losers*, based loosely on her experiences at Smith College. Not factual in any sense, the book suggests the tone and the feeling of an exclusive New England college for girls in the early sixties. Like *The Callender Papers*, this novel was also revised and published by Atheneum several years later.

Developing the Tillerman Series

While Voigt was still writing *Tell Me If the Lovers Are Losers*, the idea that began the Tillerman series came to her: "I went to the market and saw a car full of kids left to wait alone in the parking lot. As the electric supermarket doors whooshed open, I asked myself 'What would happen if nobody ever came back for those kids?' I made some jottings in my notebook, and let them stew for

Cynthia Voigt running a crab line in Chesapeake Bay with her son, Peter, in 1982.

a year, the way most of my ideas do" (Commire, 223). These notebook jottings grew into a novel twice the size of the final version of *Homecoming*, and the novel grew into six more books about the Tillermans and their friends, a series bound together by a thematic cycle of holding on, reaching out, and letting go.

In 1981, *Homecoming* was published after some severe cutting by Voigt's editor, Gail Paris, whom the author credits with the wisdom and foresight to appreciate a good book before it is finished. Although Voigt has won many awards since, she considers the acceptance of this manuscript the most important sign of recognition in her career as a writer. "After years of working on my own, I was suddenly encouraged and accepted by others. Awards are . . . presents, and while they are intensely satisfying they do not give the same kind of pleasure as being in the middle of a work that is going well" (Commire, 225). Nevertheless, Voigt received several wonderful "presents" for her first published book. *Homecoming* was selected as a Notable Children's Trade Book in the Field of Social Studies by the joint committee of the

Cynthia consulting with her daughter, Jessica, in 1983.

National Council for Social Studies and the Children's Book Council, and it was an American Book Award nominee.

Voigt was still working on *Homecoming* when she realized that she was not finished with the Tillerman family. She started *Dicey's Song* immediately afterward. Then she wrote *A Solitary Blue* to explain the character Jeff and *The Runner* to tell the story of Bullet. When she submitted *Dicey's Song* to her editor, she was not at all confident about its worth. "My cover letter read something like: I don't know that you will want this, but I think you will love reading it."[4]

After she had submitted the book, Paris asked her to write an introductory piece for readers who had not read *Homecoming*. Although Voigt complied, she was disappointed at losing her "killer first line." When the book was published, however, she was pleased to see that the publisher, by printing the introduction in a different font, had retained the original first line. "I realized that, though I hadn't said a word, Atheneum [the publisher] knew as well as I did that the first line was important" (Commire, 224). Since then, she has relied on the judgment of her publisher in much of her work.

In 1983, *Dicey's Song* won the prestigious Newbery Medal. Voigt was understandably thrilled. It had taken her over two decades of writing to see her first work published, and now to receive such an honor only two years after her first novels were in print was overwhelming. She described the experience in her Newbery Medal Acceptance speech: "I didn't know good news could pack such a wallop. I didn't know good news could keep you awake through the night, distract you so effectively from all appointed tasks, make it difficult, when you confronted it head on, to breathe properly." But she was brought back to reality by her young son: "Forty-eight hours after the famous phone call, during which time the house had been reverberating with the words Newbery and Los Angeles, we went out for a family celebration dinner. Duffle [my son] leaned forward to announce to his grandmother the big news: 'We are going to Chicago, because Mommy won the Blueberry Award.' . . . Duffle keeps my feet on the ground" (Voigt, 9).

Nineteen eighty-three was a big year for Voigt. Besides receiving the Newbery Award for *Dicey's Song*, her earlier novel *The Callender Papers* was published and awarded the Edgar Allan Poe Award, which is given to the best juvenile mystery of the preceding year. Her next novel, *A Solitary Blue*, was also released that year and named a Newbery Honor Book.

Perhaps because she had grown up in a large happy family and because she was so close to her own two children, Voigt found it especially difficult to imagine why a woman would leave her children, an important catalyst for both *Homecoming* and *A Solitary Blue*. In *Homecoming*, she justified the mother's actions by giving her a severe mental illness, while in *A Solitary Blue*, she depicted Melody as chronically immature and irresponsible. Both mothers are far from normal, yet they are quite believable because Voigt shows the root of their personal problems in their own upbringing.

Dicey's Song and *Homecoming* were books that produced other books like "shoots out of a felled tree," as Voigt explained in a commentary in 1983. Just as she wrote *A Solitary Blue* to tell Jeff's story, she wrote *The Runner* in 1985 to explain the story Gram tells the children about how Bullet got out of going to a birthday party, and then came *Seventeen Against the Dealer* to clarify the relationship of Jeff and Dicey. *Come a Stranger* (1986) explores the character development of Mina, one of Dicey's best friends, as she comes to terms with the white world's scorn of the black female body. In *Sons from Afar* Dicey's brothers, James and Sammy, redefine their relationship as they search for news about their father. The Tillerman series is perhaps Voigt's most renowned achievement, but these were not the only novels she was writing during these years.

Exploring Fate and History

In 1984, *Building Blocks* was published. This book originated in an incident in Voigt's home: "Her son Peter, who was quite young at the time, frequently played with the large, lightweight cardboard building blocks familiar to most two-year-olds. One night Walter constructed a rather large fortress with them. The next morning when Peter and Cynthia came downstairs, there it was! Peter reacted immediately and crawled into the inviting structure [and Cynthia thought], 'What would happen if . . . ?'"[5] Brann, the main character in the novel that resulted, falls asleep in the fortress built by his father and travels back into the time of his father's childhood in the Depression years. In this book, Voigt explores not only the effect of parental anxiety on children but also the nature of fate, a subject she would return to in later novels.

Jackaroo (1985) is historical fiction, set in a medieval kingdom. The main characters are peasants who struggle daily for physical survival, with little hope of improving their lot except for the sudden reappearances of Jackaroo, a mythical Robin Hood figure. Voigt calls this her "Zorro book"; indeed, it is full of flaring

Building Blocks began when Peter discovered a tower built by his father one morning.

threats and flashing swords, yet it is also astonishingly realistic in evoking this historical-mythical setting.

In 1986 Voigt wrote *Izzy, Willy-Nilly* about how a popular high school cheerleader reacts when she loses a leg as a result of a car accident. In this novel Voigt continues her campaign against mere "niceness," begun in *Tell Me If the Lovers Are Losers*, with the characterization of Ann as constrained by her fear of offending anyone—or even of being noticed. After her accident, Izzy, realizing the inadequacy of being "nice" for dealing with many real-life situations, becomes a more authentic person.

Voigt's own personality, inextricably bound up with her writing, is anything but "merely nice." When she is not writing, she claims to make a mess of things and "'get very grouchy.' It is the writing—the making of something—that helps order her world" (Kauffman, 876). Her conversation reflects her quick, insightful mind, which probes and pushes to understand the nature of life, literature, and the way they relate. Her characters are only slightly related to her own personality, though she admits that Dicey is the "kind of kid [she] would like to have been and that Gram's the kind of lady [she] would like to be." She connects to her characters with sharply focused insights into an essential part of their personalities, filling out the flesh and blood as she writes about them in the context of the novel: "You can't pin them down as to who they are, but you can connect with who they are, talk to them and see what they're trying to communicate." Voigt is drawn to her characters, but does not feel that she automatically knows all about them. "I would not be surprised if they'd all come and knock on my door and tell me I've done it all wrong" (Kauffman, 876–79).

Like her characters, the settings in her books are fictional yet related to actual pieces of own life. Her first books take place at the kind of private New England schools where she was a student. The route the children follow in *Homecoming* is familiar to anyone who has lived in southern Connecticut, and Crisfield, named after an actual town in Maryland, reflects her life in that part of the state. In a 1986 interview Voigt talked prophetically about the setting of her later novels, describing how she felt that writing about a place made it belong to her and how she dreamed of moving to Maine. Later in the year, *Stories About Rosie* was published, a picture book set in Maine, with illustrations by Dennis Kendrick. The heroine of this story is Rosie, the family dog. Soon after, the Voigts, including Rosie, became residents of that northern state.

Tree by Leaf (1988) is a historical novel set in rural Maine just after World War I. Clothilde loves the peninsula that has been willed to her. Her claim to the land she loves is threatened by her family's need for money after her father returns from the war monstrously disfigured and disowned by his wealthy family. Also set in Maine, *The Vandemark Mummy* (1991), a mystery like *The*

Callender Papers, unfolds at a small college where Dr. Hall, a classicist like Cynthia's husband Walter Voigt, has been hired to teach. Althea's knowledge of classical Greek solves the mystery, and her younger brother Phineas's persistence and courage saves her life.

In *On Fortune's Wheel* (1990), named by the American Library Association as a Best Book for Young Adults, Voigt returns to the mythical kingdom described in *Jackaroo* to tell the story of Birle, the grandaughter of Gwyn and Burl. Feeling unwanted at home, Birle runs away to the southern kingdom, is kidnapped and enslaved, escapes, and enters a life of luxury at the Court. Feeling useless and unfulfilled, she finally returns to the Inn, her grandmother Gwyn's original home, where she can pursue her work and live with her love independently.

In 1989, Cynthia Voigt received the ALAN Award from the Assembly on Literature for Adolescents, an assembly of the National Council for Teachers of English, for her significant contribution to the field of adolescent literature. In her speech acknowledging this honor, she demonstrated her talents as an English teacher when she suggested analyzing the thematic patterns in novels by mapping the plot events in each chapter (Commire, 225).

Moving Beyond Familiar Ground

Voigt's first book written expressly for adults was published in 1991. *Glass Mountain*, a light-hearted romance, takes place in the upper echelons of New York society and revolves around the struggle of two people to discern the "real self" underneath the layers of social veneer and convention. This theme reflects the growing process of Voigt's adolescent characters, who learn to look beyond the conventions of their upbringing to see the possibilities of their own self-development.

Just as Voigt explores the romantic possibilities of sophisticated high society, with its tightly defined responsibilities to its members and the manners that unite them, she also examines the tragic consequences of the underworld of evil and hatred that separates individuals from each other and undercuts the ideals of social unity. *David and Jonathan* (1992), *Orfe (1992)*, and *The Wings of the Falcon* (1993) explore these themes. In an earlier interview Voigt discussed the effect of life on her writing: "The Depression and World War II were experiences that shaped and informed me while I was growing up, just as Vietnam has influenced kids growing up today."[6] She brings these influences together in David and Jonathan and explores the long-range influences of these tragedies on the lives of two friends. *Orfe*, based on the myth of Orpheus and Eurydice (but reversing the gender positions of the protagonists), traces the poignant tragedy of a singer who cannot sustain the courage to rise above her knowledge of the world's evils. *The Wings of a Falcon* depicts the devastating effects of sadistic power on people whose struggle to survive almost erases their capacity to love. In *When She Hollers*, Voigt portrays the overpowering effects of sexual abuse of a stepfather on a young adolescent.

Voigt describes herself as someone who continues to learn rather than as someone who already knows: "If I expect myself to be learning, my attitude towards experiences, people, the whole side show, is characterized by questions and curiosity; probably more important, my understanding of who I am, myself, is that I am changing, growing, adding to myself. . . . I don't know about the rest of the adults out there, but it seems to me I spend my time perpetually growing up, with no end in sight to the arduous and uneasy occupation—which strikes me, on the whole, as a good thing, and a beneficial thing" (Commire, 225).

Voigt's recent writing shows a development toward a more profound questioning of the hard dilemmas of modern life. In *The Vandemark Mummy*, Phineas and Althea live with their father; their mother lives on the other side of the country, pursuing her own career. *David and Jonathan* deals with the separation of innocent friends when they must face the evils administered by one ethnic group on another. David had been tortured and abandoned in World War II, and Jonathan is tortured in Vietnam; Henry struggles with the guilt of being from a privileged class that does not easily acknowledge the suffering of the Jewish people, the guilt of being a noncombatant in the Vietnam War, and the shame of his attraction to his friend Jonathan. In *Orfe*, the protagonist does not have the strength to escape the underworld of drug addiction and sadism. *The Wings of a Falcon* paints the horrible impact of war, when individual lives lose their value as leaders struggle for power and others struggle to survive. *When She Hollers* describes the cruelty of fathers who use their physical and psychological strength against their weaker daughters, whose mothers cannot protect them. In these later novels, Voigt is addressing the influences of individuals made weak by evil on the lives of young people who cannot remain innocent. These are pertinent questions in a world where adolescents and children are not always safely protected by loving families from evil and isolation.

Voigt's adventures seem to be taking her farther away from an orderly surface that once was called "normal." In her later books, in their quest for the "liberation of [their] true, vital, and powerful sel[ves],"[7] her heroes challenge the traditional status quo in hopes of finding new definitions of family and society and order, just as her earlier protagonists, leaving the safety of what they knew, began to explore the world and redefine the ways they would relate to it. The style of these later works also indicates Voigt's challenge to the traditional way of telling a story to young adults. In the Tillerman series, she presented the same event and the same characters from different points of view. In *Orfe*, the characters' voices alternate, describing the same events from different points in time as well as from different points of reference. *When She Hollers* tells Tish's story through a mental dialogue that tests each assertion against logic, her memory of what others have said, and her emotional responses. Pearson and Pope describe the motivation and the effect of this style in *The Female Hero*: "The goal is to reveal the essence of the character or event. It is analogous to a process developed in consciousness-raising sessions in which one person begins by describing something she experienced and other members describe similar experiences in no particular order. The accumulation of all the individual variations on the experience makes the essence of the experience apparent."[8]

Cynthia Voigt writing in her studio.

Voigt is diving beyond the "normal" presentation of the linear causal plot in her attempt to depict the more fluid patterns of real life, where events are a compromise between logical intention and accidental fate and where conversations follow associational lines as well as chronological sequences. She is exploring the frontiers of realism in fiction in order to share her vision of how modern heroes can uncover truths about their world and the people in it, so that they may live in mutually beneficial relationships. In an

Peter, Cynthia, Walter, and Jessica and their dog, Rosie, in Maine in 1988.

interview about her writing, Voigt describes her ambition as a writer: "I don't want to tell people what to think. I want to lay out the questions. . . . A good book leads you forward . . . you're a better reader at the end of the book. If readers are curious, it's there for them; if they're not curious, they don't have to be."[9] For Voigt, what is essential for the reader is to know the book; the author's life is only incidental to the work. A good book should be "roomy," allowing plenty of space for readers to explore their responses to the elements of the book and to form their own interpretations.

2. Looking Beneath the Tip of the Iceberg: Defining the Self

In a recent autobiographical sketch, Voigt writes, "I begin to suspect that it is normal to be, like an iceberg, more than you seem to be, to be not only what you seem to be" (Gallo, 218). Her first novels portray young women in the process of defining their identities by exploring the depths of their icebound selves as they step out from the familiar environment of childhood into a world of wider experience and meet people with different lives and values. In both *The Callender Papers* and *Tell Me If the Lovers Are Losers*, Voigt describes how her protagonists overcome initial fears of the unknown and learn to judge the value and validity of their experiences with other people. They waver between two basic modes of coping with human experience: should they feel their way instinctively, using their hearts to guide them, or is logical thinking the path to understanding?

The Callender Papers (1983)

"Think carefully was the guiding principle of my upbringing,"[1] says Jean, the main character of *The Callender Papers*. This principle is embedded in her mind by her Aunt Constance, not a blood relation, but the woman who had raised her since the disappearance of Jean's parents in her infancy. The twelve-year-old girl leaves the school near Boston where she has lived as ward of the headmistress, Constance Wainwright, and spends a summer in the Berkshires organizing the family papers of Mr. Thiel, a haughty artist whom she has met only a few times. Jean is pleased that she can provide money for her future education by using her mind, though she is put off by Mr. Thiel's cold and distant nature: "He had a hard face, filled with character . . . but not attractive and not welcoming" (25). Ten years previously his wife, Irene Callender, had fallen to her death in a deep ravine from a path near the house of her brother, Enoch Callender. Their child had mysteriously disappeared shortly afterward. A few days after her arrival, Jean meets Enoch Callender, a man who immediately charms her with his sunny disposition, his sky-blue eyes and golden hair. .

In striking contrast to the iciness of Mr. Thiel, Enoch welcomes Jean, engaging her in lively conversational games, guessing her name and flattering her with his attention. Enoch tells her about his sister Irene, who had raised and spoiled him after the death of their mother, and about the fortune he hopes to inherit when the mystery of her death has been cleared. Enoch and his family have splendid dreams about how they will use the money to escape their rural isolation and live elegantly in Paris or New York. Mr. Thiel does not approve of Jean's fascination with Enoch Callender: "You want to find excuses for him" (62), he says, and she admits that she does. She is attracted to his apparent enthusiasm for life's possibilities, which contrasts sharply with the somber, emotionally constrained Thiel household, where both Mr. Thiel and his housekeeper, Mrs. Bywall, seemed suspicious of both fate and folk.

Jean discovers a lovely waterfall along the path connecting the two family houses, a welcome respite from the twelve boxes of papers she sifts through so carefully and logically. Soon after, however, she is horrified to learn that this waterfall was the site of Irene's death, perhaps not an accident but a murder, motivated by greed for the family fortune. Jean finds it difficult to imagine such a murder, for her limited experience has not introduced her to the possibilities of evil. People had always seemed kind; now she doubts that she has understood the truth about them. That night she has a nightmare. Looking down into the ravine, she sees a woman, barely alive, looking up at her. Then a tall, dark, cloaked figure grabs her away from the site. Jean screams, something she has never done before, and wakens to be awkwardly comforted by Mr. Thiel and his housekeeper, Mrs. Bywall.

Frightened by the inexplicable strength of her emotions, she resolves to face her fear by thinking carefully about the facts surrounding Irene's death and the disappearance of the child. Subsequently, her nightmares and her terror of the evil surrounding the family subside as she works diligently, poring through the boxes for clues. She is rewarded by finding references to a will that favors Irene and her child over Enoch and his family; at Irene's death the fortune was to be split between the child and Enoch. Where is this child and what name does the initial "J" signify? Jean cannot think of the answer. Why has Mr. Thiel not traced the child and tried to provide for it? Is it because he knows that the child has already died? But Mr. Thiel, the executor, is not a beneficiary and has no evident motive for murder.

A second incident arouses her fear again. Despite his disapproval of Enoch and his family, Mr. Thiel has permitted Jean to accept an invitation to dine with the Callenders at their home on Sundays. It is after one of these Sundays that Jean becomes dangerously ill with what the doctor suspects is food poisoning. Although Jean finds this illogical, she does not feel safe. She cannot decide whom to trust: the cold and distant Mr. Thiel, who is rude and overbearing but whose life has been guided by such high-minded and carefully considered moral principles, or Enoch, who, despite his profligate ways and professed wish for money, is kind and charming to her and lives with such grace. Who would want to harm her, a mere employee?

Angered by Mr. Thiel's stern manner and his injunction that she stay in the house, Jean runs to Enoch and the waterfall for comfort and to release her pent-up feelings. How can this charming, lovely man be the selfish ingrate that Mr. Thiel describes, backing up his arguments with so much logical evidence? "Things were happening too fast for careful thought" (141). Then in a flash of imagination, she realizes that "J" could stand for Jean and that she herself could be the lost child, the heiress Jean

Thiel. It makes sense, but who was greedy enough to kill Irene Thiel for the Callender fortune? Enoch had expressed such strong love for his sister, and Irene's husband could only inherit if the child was proved dead. Jean wants to deny that the cold hard-hearted Mr. Thiel must be her father, but she sees that it must be true.

Beneath Enoch's charming exterior lies a snake. As Enoch verifies what Jean has already figured out logically, he describes why she had not seen beneath his facade earlier: "You're not as clever as I had thought. You're remarkably like your mother, intelligent up to a point and then you let your feelings take over. You should guard against that, my dear" (165). But Jean has learned to recognize the importance of the heart as well as the mind in finding the truth about herself. She can use not only the stern logic of her father, Mr. Thiel, but also the imaginative heart of her mother, Irene, who in her letters had expressed such warm love toward her husband and her child. For Irene had not been unintelligent; she had recognized the evil mind beneath the sunny exterior and had been planning a will that would benefit her brother's wife and children rather than her brother himself. Enoch had been "like a distorting mirror to his children and his wife . . . like a dark cloud holding them in his shadow" (181). Despite his warm and generous exterior, he had planned to use his money to buy a munitions factory, profiting from war and destruction; although he espouses love for humanity to Jean, he had insisted on prosecuting the humble Mrs. Bywall for the theft of a spoon to pay for medicine for her dying brother, claiming principle as his motive.

Now Jean wonders what is behind the stern exterior of Mr. Thiel. "What I was looking for, precisely, I did not know. I knew only that I needed some glimpse into Mr. Thiel's heart, into my father's heart" (178). She had seen evidence in the affectionate note written by her mother that conflicted with Enoch Callender's tales about the selfish, mean-spirited nature of this man. Jean goes to Mr. Thiel's art studio, and, in the lovely painting of a woman kneeling with her child at the glade by the falls, where "sunlight washed down over them, in benediction" (179), she sees the painter's heart and weeps in admiration.

In exploring her own depths to find her identity, Jean thought she had to choose between the icy, principled logic of Mr. Thiel or the sunny, playful imagination of Enoch Callender; what she discovers is the value of both the mind and the heart, as long as they are what they seem to be.

Voigt wrote *The Callender Papers* as an exercise in plotting. This is a Gothic novel based on a dream: "I am prone to gothic dreams. . . . A gothic novel needs a plot. Write this one!"[2] Although "some of the details are historically accurate, and the diction is evocative of the period, . . . it is not a carefully researched historical piece . . . it is more a product of having read many gothic novels" (Commire, 224). As in most novels of that genre, the characters are more symbolic than full-blown personalities. Jean is a typical Victorian orphan, prim and plucky, who allays her fears of leaving her aunt with logical self-discipline. As she boards the train for the first step of her journey, she sits back "to attempt to think cheerfully" (13), determined to enjoy her adventure. Her guardian is a standard headmistress of a girl's school in Boston—a stern middle-aged woman, tall and straight with "eyes that seemed to see right to the heart of things" (3)—who represents the wise and virtuous adult. Dedicated to providing a man's education to women, Constance Wainwright's school had, beyond the usual curriculum of domestic and fine arts, "the reputation of producing suffragettes" (86). Mr. Thiel, with typical Victorian righteousness, thinks deeply about the principles that direct his life and hides his emotions along with his paintings. In contrast, Enoch seems attractively imaginative and expressive, encouraging his impressionable niece Jean to play games and learn to dance, relying on his charm to woo her affection and loyalty so he can grab her inheritance. As Jean wavers between these symbols of principled logic and profligate emotion, she finally learns the truth about her self and the people around her by thinking carefully about the information she garners from the Callender papers.

Some critics felt that the characters in this novel are unrealistically portrayed. Michelle Slung finds Jean an "unconvincingly juvenile heroine. . . . The sensibility she conveys is a rather middle-aged one."[3] Ethel Heins agrees: "Jean, so young in years, may strain the reader's credulity with her mature, self-possessed first-person account, which occasionally dips into fairly complex moral, and even philosophical, discussions."[4] Robin McKinley writes that Jean is almost "too stupid to be believed."[5] Yet Voigt's heroine reflects the Victorian era in which the novel is set, an era that discouraged immaturity and open displays of emotions, but fostered the maintenance of innocence. The stilted prose in which Jean tells her story reflects the "period primness"[6] of the Victorian era and the classical education she has received at her aunt's school. As this first novel already makes clear, one of Voigt's strengths is that her characters' personalities are consistent with the environment of their upbringing and the conventions of the historical era in which they live.

"All that glisters is not gold,"[7] and Voigt certainly uses this imagery to illustrate the theme that appearances can be deceiving. When Jean first meets Mr. Thiel, "he stood waiting in a shadow, a wide hat hiding his eyes" (13). In contrast, Mr. Callender is "a golden man" (22) in a white suit, with eyes "of blue as bright as the sky. The sun shone off of his golden hair" (48). By the end of the novel, however, she sees the darkness behind the gleaming facade of Enoch Callender and the loving glow behind Dan Thiel's cloudy countenance. Unlike Voigt's many novels that are set in real places, the geography of this novel—while suggestive of the Berkshires in western Massachusetts with its tangled woods, rocky streams, and gray boulders—is essentially fictional. In most Gothic novels, scenery and weather mirror the intention of the plot, turning gloomy in the face of impending doom. In Voigt's novel, however, the glade where Jean's mother has been murdered is welcoming to Jean; and, on the day when Enoch tries to kill her, the sun is shining, and Jean is enjoying the peacefulness of that same glade. The houses of both Thiel and Callender are of gray stone, and neither is more threatening than the other. It is in the interaction of the characters and in the mind of Jean that Voigt plays out the question of truth versus mere appearance.

Another theme of *The Callender Papers* is Voigt's belief in the importance of learning for the young heroine. Studying the family documents enables her to question the actions and motivations of other people and to test the nature of the world outside herself in order to develop a self-definition. Mr. Thiel and Jean enjoy long discussions about philosophy, exploring the ramifications of the decisions and actions of the family members. She tutors her friend Mac in Latin, building his confidence in his own ability to learn. The melodramatic plot explicitly favors thought and reflection as a road to self-development over blind acceptance of what initially appears to be true.

Tell Me If the Lovers Are Losers

In her second novel, *Tell Me If the Lovers Are Losers*, Voigt stresses human relationships, or the heart, as an equally important component of self-development. The title comes from a Carl Sandburg poem, "Cool Tombs," a poem about the release death brings from the agonies of war. As critic Claire Rosser points out, the book title has "nothing to do with romantic love; neither does this book."[8] Voigt is describing various attitudes toward life, embodied in each of her characters: the title celebrates the passionate idealism of a young girl who gives hope to her college friends even after her death.

The source for *Tell Me If the Lovers Are Losers* was a story told to Voigt when, at a dinner with friends, she tried on a pair of thick-lensed glasses and found it difficult to focus. "Knowing the owner was a basketball player, she asked, 'How do you play basketball with these?' He responded, 'No problem.' But he did recall a similar incident in high school where a 'wonderful, dead-eye shot basketball player' got glasses and could no longer play" (Kauffman, 877).

The setting is suggestive of Voigt's years at Smith College in New England in the early 1960s. Though the events of plot are not based on any actual occurrences in Voigt's college life, the tone and the feelings evoked by the variety of students meeting in an environment that encouraged independent thinking are similar. The fictional Stanton College is a small girl's school in the northeast that caters to "students of high intellectual caliber and distinct individuality."[9]

In *Tell Me If the Lovers Are Losers*, three college roommates explore the depths of their identities by asserting who they seem to be and using their differences to suggest to each other and to themselves alternate paths to try. Like Jean, Ann Gardner is pulled between two types of minds, those of her two roommates at Stanton. Ann is from a conventional upper-middle-class family, and her life has been highly controlled and ordered. Reserved, polite, and passive, she shies away from anything or anybody that is different. Unsure of her identity, Ann seeks the safety of conformity to prep school manners, familiar friends with familiar values, and privacy from challenges to her past. She hides the core of her self behind a ready smile and noncommital manners. In the beginning of the novel, Ann prefers observation to action and involvement. By the end of the novel, she has faced her fears of what lies beneath the iceberg and is well on the way to defining an identity separate from her family and friends and yet including what is valuable from them.

One of Ann's roommates is Niki Jones, whose "long face, jabbing nose and chin" and eyes that "glittered, glared" illustrate her aggressive intelligence (1). Abrasively honest in expressing her judgments, Niki uses her intellect to challenge appearances and attack discrepancies between what people say and what they do. Her pessimistic view of humanity fuels her relentless drive to control situations not by conforming and becoming invisible as Ann does, but by taking charge. During the welcoming assembly for first-year students, Niki uses a stage whisper to label the dean of students "Munchkin," dispelling the aura of respect that surrounds this paragon of scholarly seriousness. Full of energy and action, Niki spends her time playing sports and games. Her goal is to achieve the grades and the college degrees to fight for change in a society that she sees as an unjust enemy. For her, the means of winning power are less important than the end result; it is not the game that matters but the goal.

The third roommate is Hildy Koenig, tall, blonde, and strong with "a face framed for happy surprises, and . . . eyes beaming expectation" (21). Hildy is from an isolated farm in North Dakota, where she has lived a life reminiscent of pre-industrial rural America, helping her father and brothers on their chicken farm and living part-time with a neighboring widower to help with his children. Raised at a great distance from modern society, fifty miles from the nearest school and an hour away from a church, Hildy seems naive; her speech is stilted, reflecting her lack of opportunity to communicate with many people beyond her family, and her experience is limited to homely activities. But she is profoundly confident in the essential rightness of what she believes and precisely honest in explaining the extent of the knowledge. "It is the same thing, in the microscope and the telescope. The details differ, but not the essential order" (145). Hildy trusts her intuitive sense of right and wrong but fails to pay attention to the evidence of her worldly experience.

Voigt characterizes the difference between the girls' minds metaphorically. Niki's mind can be like fire, sudden, "crackling and destructive" (97). A quick, erratic learner, she is more interested in the factual certainties of math and science than in probing human motives and ideas. Valuing the facts and things of the material world, she is a pedestrian writer, producing safe, correct prose for the sake of a grade rather than to express or explore ideas. In contrast, Hildy is interested in broad spiritual truths. She sees life in large, generous patterns, gleams of light against darkened shadows. Her mind, solid and almost unalterable is "like a large forest, too complex, too tough . . . for garden management; . . . what you planted would be altered by the nature of the forest into something other than you had imagined" (94). Ignorant of many facts and details about sophisticated modern life, she is nevertheless perceptive about people and sure about questions of right and wrong. Although she lacks an adequate academic background to succeed, Hildy registers for astronomy and biology because she wants to know more of what they offer.

Curious about the contrary extremes of Niki's worldly pragmatism and Hildy's fuzzy idealism, and jealous of the certainty of both of her roommates, Ann is cautious at first: "Like a string of real pearls around her neck, in the dark of night on the wrong street, she nervously concealed her mind, her unquiet fingers both cherishing and proud" (48). Ann loves literature, the lovely patterns of imagery, meaning, and sound that words can create. She loves the ideals of excellence that she finds, particularly in classical literature. But at the beginning of the novel she conceals this love, afraid of being teased or envied. Ann's mind was water, "a lake held within controlling banks, sensitive to induced changes, but always with unexpected water-promises. . . . You could easily see how to improve a lake, although you could not predict what it might give up to you from its unseen depths" (94). She writes carefully, placing "fact atop fact [to build] an impregnable wall" (96). Ann's desire to be invisible has constrained her interactions with other people: she has snubbed square-bodied, square-faced Eloise without finding out that her mind was anything but square and that she could be an excellent friend.

As the roommates share their work and cooperate in their learning, Ann begins to assert her intellect, showing Hildy how to use the quote from the play she is studying to back up her intuitions about the characters' motivations and challenging Niki to work harder to develop and express her own opinions. Niki begins to listen to Ann, recognizing her excellent logic, and begins to respect Hildy's devotion to her high moral ideals.

It is on the volleyball courts that the differences among the three roommates are played out most dramatically. At first, Ann does not play, preferring to sit on the sidelines, observing Hildy and Niki as they express their contrary personalities. "The game became schizoid: on Hildy's side the ball was gentled, made soft; on Niki's it was energized and pointed" (40). Niki is individual and competitive, grabbing points, yelling at her teammates to keep out of her way. In constrast, Hildy cares most about cooperating as a team, retrieving and passing the ball until a point can be made. When Niki suggests that she and Hildy could join the first-year team and play together in order to win the tournament,

Hildy refuses at first. She accuses Niki of allowing her emotions to dominate not only her own actions but the play of her team. Eventually, all three join four other first-year girls to forge a team. Ann agrees to play volleyball in order to keep peace between her roommates. Hildy, now a part-time coach, inspires the girls to think of themselves as a team.

One evening as they continue practicing into the twilight, the girls realize that they can play without looking at each other, simply by sensing the game's pattern and by supporting each other's plays as integral parts of the pattern. Niki shows Ann how to spike, hone her skills, and play more aggressively. The team wins against the other first-year teams, but when they play against the sophomores, they begin to fall apart. "We should win this match, but we cannot if we *expect* to lose it," advises Hildy, and her confident vision carries them to victory: "the opposing team creaked, cracked, and crumbled" (98–99).

Though Hildy's communal vision inspires the team, her eyesight has been the subject of much concern to Niki and Ann. Both have noticed that Hildy holds her books almost next to her nose, but they have not been able to convince her to get her eyes examined. Part of the problem, Ann discovers, is that Hildy has only ten dollars to spend for the whole year. Goaded by Niki to act instead of passively giving up, Ann approaches the Dean and suggests that the college pay Hildy for her coaching. Hildy still refuses the examination until Ann blows up in anger after saving Hildy from falling over a waterfall she did not see.

Hildy's eyes are very poor. Nearsighted in one eye and farsighted in the other, she has seen only blurred outlines and shapes without defining outlines; these are normal to her. With her glasses, however, she develops an opposite problem, seeing too clearly the "clutter" of the world. During the next volleyball match, Hildy cannot concentrate. Watching the ball and the faces of the other players, her timing is off. Her grace and her confidence are impaired. Fiercely determined to win, Niki relentlessly threatens and wills the players to compensate for Hildy's new weakness, and they do, but not with any joy. The game with the juniors starts badly, as Ann and the others strain while the juniors play easily and well. Hildy, frustrated at her own inept timing, hurls her glasses into the stands and begins to play with her former grace. Without her glasses, Hildy is not distracted by details: "It is all soft, smooth, simple. I see what will happen and what has happened. The ball floats to me, like a little cloud. . . . There is no winning, no losing, just the play itself" (151). The freshmen team relaxes and finally wins because they believe they can.

Hildy agrees to compromise, wearing her glasses except for when she plays volleyball. But with her glasses, Hildy increasingly notices petty flaws in people, judging now what she had previously ignored. She sees beyond the shadowy images and gleams of light, and her idealized image of her world is compromised. Her confidence is shaken. She perceives the vanity of Beth, whom she had previously considered "a sulky goddess . . . who needed to honor herself" (140). With her glasses she also notices that Niki has written a paper based on Ann's ideas about King Lear—not a technical plagiarism, but a borrowed idea nonetheless. She is convinced that Niki has committed a moral wrong. Niki responds that what she has done is legal and that being right is a matter of winning, of having the power to define what is right. With unassailable logic, she accuses Hildy of being as self-serving and as "human" as herself, admirable but no more capable of defining a meaning of life than anyone else. Hildy is unable to accept such an assault on her innocence. Abandoning her glasses forever, she bikes out on an icy road that she cannot clearly see and is killed by a driver whose sight is also impaired, in this case by alcohol. Tragically, Hildy misses knowing that Niki has rewritten her paper, respecting Hildy's idealistic faith in humanity and trying to make amends for pushing her harsh logical facts into Hildy's mind.

Ann has grown confident in her ability to modify Niki's pessimism. While Niki's characterization of life as meaningless and vile may be true in some cases, it is also true that life, lived well, may have meaning and excellence. Niki has learned to trust Ann's eye for excellence and to care about her opinion. Daring to face their fears, Niki and Ann have learned to accept what is valuable in each other, and to accept their new roommate Eloise too. For their four remaining years at Stanton the volleyball team, built by Hildy's vision of cooperative play, remains undefeated.

What had seemed impossible happens. Ann and Niki and the other girls, too, have learned to explore beneath their iceberg tips and plunge to new depths using both mind and hearts, to define themselves as strong individuals who also work together toward the ideal of a stronger team. Ann recognizes the worth of standing up for her views as well as of loyalty to friends and family. Niki recognizes the importance of striving toward an ideal of excellence as well as tearing down facades. Perhaps Hildy, had she lived, could have learned to incorporate the faults and failings of her friends into her idealized vision of humanity. Perhaps the warmth of Niki's gesture of respect and devotion and of Ann's invitations to join her family would have melted the hardness of the categorical imperatives that bound her mind. In any case, as the title from Sandburg's poem implies, her love for greater ideals had a lasting impact on her friends and teammates who became winners, and that makes Hildy a winner too; like heroes in classical tragedies, her life has made the world a better place. For, as Niki had pointed out, "Winners are right by definition. They have the power to make themselves right" (167).

This novel opens with the words, "In 1961, the first hopeful year of John F. Kennedy's presidency, Stanton College opened its doors to the forty-first freshman class" (1). Perhaps Voigt is telling this story as a metaphor for that generation of young people whose idealistic vision of a new era in American history brought them together for a while to work as a team to try to forge a society that was more inclusive than the past social hierarchies. Like others who were shocked by the president's death, Ann is confused and distraught for a while by the death of Hildy, who had come to symbolize the hope for a better world. But she, like other young people whose vision of a new harmony was tarnished by the stark realities of death and war, gets back into the game, saddened but wiser. "She knew better than to forget, or want to. . . . No blind peace" (198). She could face "Niki's vision of the world, chaotic and accidental—brutish . . . construct[ed] out of cruel facts" because of "that sense of strength and the mystery of human love" that is "Hildy's vision, an armor of faith, . . . certain of the answers to questions that are better not asked, sure of direction if not destination" (190).

In this novel and in her later works, Voigt affirms the importance of facing even the harsh and chaotic facts of life, of reaching out toward the truth. But she indicates that stark reality cannot be faced alone; it is also important to hold on to "the ties of need and responsibility and affection, and of blood" (190) that Ann, like Jean of *The Callender Papers*, finds in family and friends, even if their purpose and meaning is not fully understood.

The style of this novel is philosophical and thoughtful. The dialogue is complex and "filled with introspection,"[10] and sounds like exceptionally intelligent conversation. Although there is some reference to the characters' impressions of President Kennedy, not much is made of the historical period except for the portrayal of Ann's family as conservative and family-oriented. The main imagery concerns Hildy's defective sight, and her reluctance to use glasses that force her to perceive the details around her with disturbing clarity.

Some critics find this "heavy going and sluggish, . . . thick with philosophy"[11] or melodramatic and excessively theatrical with exaggerated characterizations.[12] Because the novel was published immediately after the award-winning *Dicey's Song*, it is likely that it suffers by comparison, and it is generally recommended only for older adolescents.

The search for identity and self-awareness is central to all of Voigt's novels, yet personal fulfillment is never achieved without a journey into the mind and heart of others. In the process of defining an individual identity, Voigt's protagonists search for a balance between stretching the mind toward new adventures and retaining what the heart holds dear. Finally, Voigt's works probe the many layers of reality behind what appears to be evident, breaking the ice of fear, ignorance, and prejudice to reveal the exciting depths of human possibility.

3. Reaching Out, Holding On, and Letting Go: Self-Development in Cynthia Voigt's Tillerman Series[1]

Cynthia Voigt's series about the Tillerman family begins with four children's search for a home in *Homecoming* and ends with their entrance into the adult world in *Seventeen Against the Dealer*. The Tillerman saga traces the paths of these children and their friends as they develop the insight, expend the effort, and gather the courage to dare to become mature young adults, capable of making choices about the people they will love and the work they will do.

In these seven novels, Voigt describes how characters escape from damaged relationships by *reaching out* beyond themselves, *holding on* to the natural strengths of familial bonds, and finally *letting go* of ties that imprison—themes, Voigt says, that ran through her mind like a recurrent tune as she was writing the Tillerman story (Commire, 223). It is in writing this series that Voigt clarifies her ideas about the cyclical process of her characters' self-development. Throughout the Tillerman saga, Voigt brings these themes of self-discovery and self-development to life with three motifs that recur in a cyclic rhythm: singing, wood, and sailing. The Tillermans and their friends learn to reach out through the music they make, hold on through contact with wood, and let go by sailing out onto the sea. These metaphoric images appear in varying degrees in each of the Tillerman novels.

31

Homecoming (1981)

Homecoming traces the journey of Dicey and her younger brothers and sister from the Rhode Island shopping mall where they are abandoned by their mother, many miles from their home in Provincetown, Massachusetts, to Crisfield on the eastern shore of Maryland, where they find a home with their grandmother. Dicey, thirteen and often mistaken for a boy, is tough, independent, practical, and fiercely loyal to her family. James, ten, is intelligent both with book-sense and with the common-sense of asking the right questions for the situation. Maybeth, nine and a pretty blonde, has intuitive knowledge of people, but she thinks and speaks slowly, and is in danger of being labeled "retarded." The youngest, Sammy, six, is stubbornly aggressive and enthusiastically cheerful by turns; he is sturdy and physically adept, the natural athlete of the family. The distinct personalities of these Tillerman children unfold as they seek a home and mature throughout the series.

Although their mother, Liza, is no longer capable of caring for her children, the songs she has taught them sustain their hope as they try to survive on their own. Asleep in the parking lot where their mother abandoned them, Dicey, now in charge as the oldest, wakes to the sound of her youngest sister Maybeth "singing softly, one of Momma's songs, about making her love a baby with no crying."[2] Maybeth, mentally slow like their mother but instinctively sensitive to the emotional aura of a situation, recognizes the needs of the children. Practical and earthbound, Dicey is the strength of the family, squarely facing the fact that her mother will not return, feeding her family, and starting to plan their future. But later, after their first day of walking, when life seems impossible, it is again Maybeth who comforts: "It's all right, Dicey. . . . I'm going to sing" (28). When the children seem most defeated and split apart by exhaustion and tension, singing brings them back to each other.

The words of the Tillermans' songs give clues to their story. In her article, "A Newbery Song for Gifted Readers," Eliza Dresang discusses the relevancy of the song-lyrics to the plot in *Dicey's*

Song; and we may extend this thesis to the other novels. The folk song "Pretty Polly," which the Tillerman children also sing in *Homecoming*, tells the story of a young mother who dies after being deserted by her man. The children do not recognize this song as prophecy and merely feel content in the mutual warmth of making music. Later, however, the words of another song bring both comfort and a helpful message. Stuck on the wrong side of the Connecticut River, in sight of a bridge that is impossible to walk across, Dicey is lost in despair. "Was this how Momma felt?" she wonders. As she imagines her mother's feelings of helplessness, she remembers a song that her mother used to sing: "The water is wide, I cannot get o'er. Neither have I wings to fly. . . . Give me a boat that will carry two, and two shall row—my love and I" (80). As the song dispels her worry and allows her to reach out in thought to the others, Dicey becomes receptive to the musical solution of her problem. They "borrow" a rowboat and row across.

Singing is also the way the Tillermans connect to the people they meet, and each song reflects the singer's character and impact on the children's moral development. In *Homecoming*, the Tillerman children pass time at a beach resort with a couple of vagrant teenagers, Louis and Edie. Edie has an autoharp and plays "Pretty Peggy-O." "But this wasn't their song. This song was about William the false lover and how he tricked pretty Peggy-O into running away with him but then murdered her. Edie sang the song quick and cruel, with sharp metallic sounds from her instrument" (57). "You're a good singer," says James, but Louis and Edie do not turn out to be good people, not innocent like Momma. After an evening of lively dancing with Maybeth, Sammy, and James, this furtive couple slips off at the first sign of a police car. Apparently Louis has induced the more innocent Edie to run off with him, suggesting that the song is prophecy. The sinister air of this couple infects the children, for at this park Sammy steals first food and then a wallet, and James exaggerates the effects of a head injury, failing to be honest to Dicey. The vagrants' singing in this seaside resort reflects a moral laxity, as the children succumb to easy stolen pleasures and falsehoods. It has been a place of physical rest but also moral danger.

The children learn a contrary lesson when they meet two Yale students in New Haven. The garrulous, generous Windy offers to help Dicey as she sits forlorn on a wet park bench, and he buys food for the hungry children. His roommate Stewart is more serious and thoughtful about moral issues. This time, when James steals money, rather than excusing it as justifiable as had Louis and Edie, Stewart teaches James the concept of personal integrity. Stewart produces his Dobro, a traditional folk instrument, as Maybeth agrees to sing. Though "Greensleeves" is another song about abandonment in love, the perspective now shifts from the false gaiety of the murderous lover to the righteous sorrow of the one betrayed: "Alas, my love, you do me wrong, to cast me off discourteously" (103). Then Stewart teaches Maybeth another song that will be repeated in Dicey's mind throughout the Tillerman books: "Oft I sing for my friends, When death's dark form I see. / When I reach my journey's end, who will sing for me?" (104) The song affirms friendship as a bond that gives solace against the final separation of death. The time spent at Yale is beneficial for the children, and morally instructive for James, who will eventually return as a student.

During their wanderings, Dicey's goal had been Bridgeport, Connecticut, where she hoped to find a home for her sister and brothers with her aunt, the only relative her Momma had ever mentioned. But when they reach the house in Bridgeport, their aunt is dead; only her daughter Eunice remains, and there is no singing. Prim and fearful, Cousin Eunice only goes through the motions of reaching out, either because duty is all she is capable of, or because, at heart, she does not want to have the children live with her. Dicey knows that she must find another place to stay when she sees Maybeth sitting outside the circle of girls on the playground, not doing the one thing that is easy and lovely to her, singing. "It was as if Maybeth wasn't even there, not even to herself" (154). Music is the measure of Maybeth's mental health: "She learns songs fast, music and words. She couldn't be retarded and do that, could she?" (152) The Tillerman children leave

Bridgeport, and two days later, Maybeth is humming Stewart's song, "Oft I sing for my friends," reaching out again (180).

Wood is a metaphor Voigt uses for the theme of holding on. In an interview in 1983, she described the importance of wood: "Wood is like water; it's one of those things that is so responsive to humans. It's like a living metaphor. Wood has the grain; it has the color; and it's never quite the same. It can be shaped into many things. You can touch it with your hands and it has a certain warmth to it. . . . You're in touch with something that's more real and permanent than you are—although not necessarily more true. It's like standing next to something that's contagiously good" (Metzger and Straub, 470).

Just as singing is the image and the means of reaching out to dispel alienation of the self, wood is Voigt's metaphor for holding on to the verities of family, home, and fellow humanity. Wood is a natural living substance, traditionally used to symbolize that which is rooted and yet keeps on growing—the family tree, the tree of knowledge that distinguishes humanity from the animal world.

Dicey's first home was in Provincetown on the beach, nestled among the dunes, but "if you took home to mean where you rested content and never wanted to go anywhere else, Dicey had never had a home . . . ; the ocean made her restless" (*Homecoming*, 85): it was a home without roots. As the children travel, occasionally they find resting places among trees, where they feel more like a family than otherwise, but the image of wood does not become strong until they find their home in Crisfield. In Bridgeport the house they found did not prove to be a home. Its plastic, artificial surfaces were "shiny clean. The gray lineoleum floor gleamed, the refrigerator shone, the windows looking over a tiny yard, were polished. There was a formica-topped table in the center of the room" (113). After the police, urged by Eunice, locate their mother in a Boston mental hospital, now catatonic and apparently unconscious of life around her, Dicey hears Eunice discussing plans for their future, plans that threaten to separate the children. Armed with the address of another relative, their grandmother who lives on a farm on the eastern shore of Maryland, the children run away again, this time on a bus to Annapolis. From there they hitch a ride across the bay on a sailboat, and Dicey discovers what she wants to do with her life.

For Dicey, sailing is an image of freedom. The ocean is a road that never ends, always moves (*Dicey's Song*, 1). It is not home, and it makes Dicey restless (*Homecoming*, 85). It never freezes, always smashing up the little ridges of ice that form along its edges (*Dicey's Song*, 138), and so it never traps a person. To have a sailboat or to be a sailboat seems a way to let go of the constraints of responsibility and to take chances, to travel without plans, whichever way the wind blows: "A boat could be a home. The perfect home that could move around, a home that didn't close you in or tie you down," thinks Dicey the first time she sails (*Homecoming*, 199). After the long summer of reaching out for her family and to her family in order to hold on, "Dicey didn't feel like finding a harbor. She knew she needed one, and they needed one, but she would rather sail along." She realizes, however, that "life isn't really an ocean and she wasn't really a little boat bobbling along on it. There were James and Maybeth and Sammy" (199–200).

The children continue walking toward Crisfield. When they stop to earn money by picking tomatoes, the farmer threatens them physically, using a large hungry dog to keep them from continuing their journey. They are saved when Dicey puts the farmer's truck in gear, distracting him from the chase, and when the dog, rather than following them, stops to eat the biscuits they have dropped. When the farmer pursues them the next day, they escape into a circus tent, and in a wonderfully dramatic scene they are rescued by Claire, a tiny dog-trainer who has a way with her whip. Just as the children had made the final leg of their journey to Bridgeport in the car of their savior from Yale, now the owner of the circus drives them to Crisfield.

In contrast to the pristine house in Bridgeport, their future home in Crisfield is faded white clapboard, neglected, with a wooden door. The long table is "made of wood and . . . scrubbed to a pale, smooth finish" (247). The paperwood mulberry tree growing next to the house, with its four trunks held together by strong twisted wires to keep the weight of growing branches from pulling the tree apart, becomes a metaphor for their family and, later, a resting place for their mother. Here is the home they will "hold on to."

When Dicey discovers a sailboat in the barn of her grandmother's farm, she decides that the boat will be her prize if they can stay, her prize for holding on until the family finds a home. When Dicey finally does put the boat into the water, it sinks; but she remains calm as she plans the next step. "Dicey doesn't mind, as long as she knows what to do about things,"[3] explains Maybeth. Dicey does not know enough yet to be able to let go safely; she still has a lot to learn about reaching out in order to hold on. For now, working on the boat in the barn, scraping off the old paint and sanding it, offers Dicey respite from the constraints of taking care of her family. She escapes to the barn and begins to relax enough to learn about reaching out.

Dicey's Song (1982)

Dicey's Song is the story of how Dicey reaches out beyond the small circle of her family, finally able to share the responsibility for her sister and brothers with Gram, finally sure enough of her home to reach out, first to Jeff through music, and then to Mina and others through her own medium, writing. Now that some of her responsibilities for her sister and brothers is shared by her grandmother, Dicey becomes aware of her own developing maturity, both physical and emotional. Again, music is the metaphor for "reaching out" for all of the characters. Music brings Maybeth to life, and music introduces the first adult friend into the family's life. After Bridgeport, the children finally reach Crisfield and their grandmother, a fierce and independent woman who has chased her own children away as described in *The Runner*. When Dicey convinces her to let them stay, they gradually form a family. Gram grudgingly dares to reach out to Mr. Lingerle, the music teacher, first for Maybeth's sake as she swallows her pride and

accepts his offer of extra piano lessons, and then also for his sake
as she recognizes his need for them. Her insight turns out to be
correct, for as the novels progress, Mr. Lingerle benefits from the
family's adventures, just as they benefit from his generous help
in times of emergencies.

Dicey tells a friend that she chooses people by their courage
and their music, which, for her, signifies their ability to reach
out. Indeed, she meets Jeff by listening to his music; they will
eventually marry. After her initial aloofness, she joins him in
song, and it is through music that Jeff is introduced into the
Tillerman family. Eventually he brings his guitar to their house
and gets Maybeth to sing. James and his new friend Toby overcome their awkwardness by discussing the words to the songs
with Jeff, and soon Dicey's new friend, Mina, comes by and adds
her alto. This scene illustrates the Tillermans' emergence from
the silent desolation of the previous generation to the noisy conversation of the current family, who are beginning to connect
with each other as well as with a network of friends. Music has
helped provide the courage and the confidence to build these
bridges.

In the course of their first few months together, Dicey works at
the grocery store with Millie, a slow-minded but wise former
schoolmate of Abigail Tillerman, and through her she learns
some of her grandmother's background. Dicey also suffers the
humiliation of being accused of plagiarizing a story she has written about her mother; Mina's defense of Dicey's honesty cements
the beginning of their friendship, which spans many years.
Sammy worries Dicey because he fights, infuriated by the insult-
ing remarks his schoolmates make about his grandmother—until
she comes to the school one day as the Lone Marble Ranger, and
wins their respect. Dicey and James and Gram solve their problems by thinking hard, by using their minds to come up with
imaginative new possibilities for solutions to their poverty and to
the isolation their differences cause them in social situations.
The plot of *Dicey's Song* hangs more on the development of the
Tillermans into capable and loving individuals than on any single
event.

Soon after Gram signs adoption papers, the family is notified that their mother is dying. Gram and Dicey travel to Boston, and, after her death, bring back her ashes in a wooden box chosen by Dicey, crafted by a man whose hands have "cuts like the grains of the different woods" (180). Dicey's hands hold the box on the long train ride south from Boston to Crisfield. She is holding on to her memories of her mother as she is holding on to her ashes in the wooden box.

Even as Dicey is clinging to the memories of her life before Crisfield, she is also letting go. Though her hands are wrapped around the wooden box that contain the ashes of her Momma, she feels "as if she were a sailboat and the sails were furled up now, the mainsail wrapped up around the boom, and she was sitting at anchor. It felt good to come to rest. . . . But a boat at anchor wasn't planted there, like a tree. Furled sails were just waiting to be raised, when the sailor chose to head out again" (187). Later, Dicey will become a builder of boats, a career that symbolizes her combined desires to hold on with wood and to sail free.

A Solitary Blue (1983)

A Solitary Blue also begins with a mother abandoning her progeny, but this mother has money, family, and a mind that is quick and facile; she abandons her only son, seven-year-old Jeff, and her professor husband to pursue a succession of charitable causes that seem more important than love and loyalty to particular people. Afraid that he will also lose his father, a professor who devotes himself to academics, Jeff tries so hard to keep from disturbing his schedule that he loses any sense of being a self. Four years after his mother's departure, he spends an enchanted summer with his mother at her homeplace in Charleston, where he is given an identity as "the last in a long line of Boudrault men."[4] Because his mother, aptly named Melody, plays the guitar, Jeff decides to emulate her and spends the ensuing year struggling to learn the instrument. During that winter, his father, "the professor," tries to reach out to him by giving him a Martin, a classic guitar. Jeff appreciates the professor's efforts, yet, still enamored of his mother's flashes of warmth, he yearns to see her again.

The next summer Jeff discovers that, as with most of her other commitments, his mother has abandoned music and him again for something new. He finally expresses his anger toward his mother, but she acts as if this first honest feeling of his is unimportant. Feeling deeply hurt and utterly alone in his world, Jeff gradually learns to row and finally reaches a sea island where he spends the night. There he painfully lets go of his belief in his mother and, by forgetting, finds an opening within himself where he can mentally escape. Unlike Dicey, who wants to build and preserve her boat, Jeff smashes this one so no one else will ever own it. At this point in his life he decides that, rather than risk the pain of rejection again, he will hold on to nothing except this memory, this opening inside him.

In this episode, there seems a strong correlation between the theme of letting go and the symbol of the smashed boat. Back in Baltimore with his father, Jeff buries himself in this island memory to protect himself from further hurt, ignoring school and the rest of life around him. Increasingly concerned about his son's frequent absences from school, both mental and physical, the professor clumsily helps Jeff to overcome his inner fears and to reach out again. Jeff takes up playing the old wooden guitar again, and discovers that he plays better than his mother, who never practiced enough to gain a lasting skill. It is through his guitar playing that he meets Dicey Tillerman and her family.

The title *A Solitary Blue* refers to the great blue heron that Jeff first sees on his trip to the sea island outside of Charleston and then again when he and the professor search for a home on the eastern shore. In both places the ungainly heron, although nervous, remains near Jeff, letting him be there too; it represents mutual tolerance of the characters' innermost needs for honest respect. By the time Jeff meets his mother for the last time, after he has inherited the Boudrault wealth in the shape of a large diamond ring, Jeff has recognized that he has inside him his own "solitary blue," a part of himself that stands apart and watches him with self-tolerance and self-respect. In the novel's final scene, Melody asks Jeff to give her the diamond ring, which she will sell, and tosses him the jade ring that represents the more enduring heritage of the Boudrault family. Jeff recognizes that, while his mother is expert in reaching out and letting go, she has never learned to hold on to what is truly valuable.

The Runner (1985)

The Runner reaches back to the 1960s to explain some of Gram's bitterness and reluctance to accept her grandchildren and to trace the source of their mother's failure to thrive. The original Tillermans, Abigail Hackett and her husband, John Tillerman, live isolated on a farm with their three children, John Jr., Samuel ("Bullet"), and Liza. The father walls himself in further with books and ideas, becoming self-righteous and cruelly stern. Similarly the mother Abigail, immured in a passive sense of duty that keeps her from reaching out, has let her children get away from her. Her eldest son, John, has fled to California, letting go and holding on to nothing; Bullet, buried in anger and hatred, feels boxed in by his family. Liza has reached out and given life through her lovely singing, but she is not strong enough to cope with the irresponsible wanderings of the children's father, Francis Verricker, whom she never marries. As the reader learns in *Homecoming*, she is unable to handle parenthood alone and eventually abandons her children in a parking lot. *The Runner* tells the story of Gram's younger son, Sam, called "Bullet," who, like his sister Liza, cannot hold on—whose father's unbending hate and the passive nonresistance of his mother forbid him from "reaching out" and keep them from "holding on." Long ago, before he left for college, his brother Johnny had built a sailboat and a treehouse, but Bullet's anger makes him a "breaker." Rather than fix the barn door he smashes it, and he lacks the patience to sand the lovely wooden boat, the fourteen-footer, that his employer and mentor, Patrice, is building.

Bullet tries to dispel some of his anger at his father's dictatorial demands by running. The book realistically portrays both the difficult effort of long-distance running as well as the therapeutic satisfactions it provides. In school he remains aloof from the controversies about the Vietnam draft and the recent integration of the school, participating only in the cross-country team, where he helps lead the school to success. His best friend is Patrice, an older oyster-man who has emigrated from France. Patrice reconstructs sailboats, lovingly restoring the beauty of the original wood, just as he tries to rebuild Bullet, who is buffeted by "the old wind in the old anger" (174, 185) of his father and of his own racial and social prejudices. When Bullet discovers that the friend he admires so much is dark tan–colored because of his African-American heritage as well as because of his love of the sunny outdoors, he has to rethink his racial prejudices. Reluctantly he agrees to help train the new runner on the team, an intelligent black student named Tamer Shipp, who is trying to earn a scholarship for college. Bullet comes to respect Tamer's grit and determination, and, although he himself signs up to fight in Vietnam, elicits a promise from Tamer that he will avoid the draft.

Bullet is afraid of being boxed in by his father's stern orders, by fear, or even by his feelings for his sister Liza (94). He cannot "reach out" himself and connect; he cannot "hold on" and remain in his home; but he does finally see a way to enable his mother to survive. In blatant defiance of his father's orders, Bullet sits down at the table to eat with his mother and father. When his father protests, "the anger pouring out of [him], blowing all around him: go away, go away," Bullet sits firm and calm: "It's her table too" (153, 154). His father lets it go. Bullet wins the battle, holding the remains of his family together if just for an evening. The wooden table where they eat "had been put together the same way that fourteen-footer had, somebody's best work. It was as old as the farmhouse" (154). The table reunites Bullet with his mother, Abigail, in this episode just as it unites Abigail and her grandchildren years later in *Dicey's Song*. Bullet does his best when running at the next cross-country meet, and his mother slips away from the farm to watch him, to let him know she cares more than she can say.

On his eighteenth birthday, Bullet drops out of school, enlists, and buys the fourteen-foot sailboat to give to his mother. The boat that she had been using, the sailboat that her older son Johnny had made long ago, is rotting, uncared for by her husband, who does not sail, and by herself because she lacks the strength to take it out of the water each year. Bullet then dismantles the old sails, scrapes the hull, and carefully stores it in the barn, where Dicey will discover it on her first day in Crisfield. Bullet is not able to work with wood himself, "to hold on" in his own life, but he can provide the means for his mother. He cannot get her out of her own box, but he can "loosen a board or two for her" (174).

Bullet dies in Vietnam. When his mother hears the news, she takes the phone to town and throws it through the plate glass window of the telephone company. Then she strides back to the boat: "What was that song Liza sang? 'The water is wide, cannot get o'er,' the voice in her head sang, 'And neither have I wings to fly. Bring me a boat—' Well she had the boat. And the wide water ran, she knew, around the whole world, ringing it around, the encircling oceans that somehow contained and connected all the lands within" (181). The wood that symbolizes "holding on" can be crafted into a vessel that supports the sailor as he or she "lets go" and, secure in his own humanity, connects with the adventure of humanity at large.

Come a Stranger (1986)

Ten years later, *Come a Stranger* explains how Wilhemina (Mina) Smiths has come to terms with being a member of a black minority in a white society. She is proud and ambitious after a summer at an exclusive ballet school in New England where she has earned a scholarship, learning more about music, dance, and the world outside Crisfield than she had known existed. Music has enabled her to "reach out" of her rural black family-centered world. After that first summer, she is even a little scornful of the cultural limitations of Crisfield and lives in anticipation of the next summer, when she can return to the magic of ballet. The music stops, however, when she realizes that the camp needed her only as a representative of the black race and that, in this second summer, she is no longer welcome as an equal. During the winter, her body has matured into the curves indigenous to her family and some of her race so that she no longer fits into the traditional white world of ballet and is asked to leave. She is devastated. Needing something to hold onto, she turns to wood: "She wanted to put her palms up against the bark of the trees, to feel how strong and solid the trees were . . . , to get back in touch with those things that didn't look at her and see just the outside Mina" (49). After she returns home, her new friendship with Tamer Shipp, who has now finished school and become a minister, helps her learn to accept herself and her people as strong and beautiful: "The faces were all the colors of wood, seasoned and stained, oak and pecan, maple and pine" (74). This is a world she will hold on to. She understands the image of the tree that bleeds, the punishment in Dante's Hell for those who despised their own bodies enough to kill themselves. She finally accepts herself as she is, knowing the strength of her mind and her courage to learn, holding on to what and whom she has, and using these strengths to reach out in new directions. A few years later, now a confident leader in her school, Mina reaches out to Dicey, who has just arrived in Crisfield. Breaking through the fierce reserve of the Tillermans, she becomes an important friend to the family.

Sons from Afar (1987)

In *Sons from Afar*, James Tillerman also feels like a stranger. More intellectual than his classmates, he tries to hide his true nature in order to fit in; as a result, however, he feels dishonest and cowardly and confused about who he really is. Driven by these questions and hoping that his father's identity will help him define his own, James manipulates his brother Sammy into joining him on a quest for facts about the father whom he barely

remembers and whom Sammy has never known. The search carries them first to Cambridge, Maryland, to a third-grade teacher
who remembers their father, Francis Verricker, as bright and
intelligent, mischievous but a natural leader. The high school
principal remembers their father differently, recalling a cheating
troublemaker whom he enjoyed throwing out of school. Finally,
the boys' quest leads them to a seedy bar in Baltimore, where
some merchant seamen identify their father as a man who
reneges on his promises and debts, a fun-loving man with no
staying power. The seamen take out their frustration with Verricker on James and Sammy with curses, insults, and finally fists.

Purged of their own anger by this dangerous brawl, Sammy
and James return to Crisfield, fearing that they may have inherited Verricker's inability to do anything right for long. Yet within
the context of their family and with the help of their newfound
friendships, both learn to play out their strengths and become
better men than the father who lost his way. The imagery in this
book centers on stars, the moon, and exploring, as the boys work
out their definitions of fatherhood; stars are distant pin-pricks of
light that Sammy would like to explore, looking constant like
James' hopeful image of fathers: "always there, they don't
change" (13). Dicey knows, however, that the stars that had
made their light millions of years ago "already were burning with
new light" (*Dicey's Song*, Prologue). She has no desire to renew
the memory of the father who had abandoned them so long ago.
And before she died, her moon-faced mother lay in a hospital bed,
her visage "flat and empty, so far away, as if it hung miles above
the earth and could not be bothered by anything happening on
the little planet below" (*Homecoming*, 163). Like the stars, which
seem so near and yet actually are so far away, their relationship
to their father and mother sheds only a faint light on who they
might become.

In *Sons from Afar*, music again acts as a metaphor for reaching
out of oneself. Although Maybeth reaches out to her schoolmates
as a member of the chorus, James is afraid to join because he
thinks singing would emphasize his image as a "dork." Only
when he learns to accept himself and gains the courage to be

himself does he decide to join the singing group. He and Sammy sing together, partly to watch over Maybeth. The words of the songs in *Homecoming* and *Dicey's Song* tell the story of Liza, the mother of Dicey, James, Sammy, and Maybeth and the only daughter of Gram. In *Sons from Afar*, the song from Shakespeare's *The Tempest*, "Full fathom five thy father lies," is perhaps the real news about their father, either literally or figuratively: "Of his bones are coral made. . . . Nothing of him but doth change" (46). The mystery of their father's character and his whereabouts is never solved for the Tillermans. In *The Runner* he is introduced as a figure who plays music on the jukebox and gets people to have fun for a time, but he does not join in himself nor does he commit himself to others. For his children, he is forever absent.

Singing and music not only reach out, but they invite others to join in. Liza and her youngest daughter, Maybeth, are naturally generous; Dicey and the other children learn to join in the music and the world. Their success contrasts with those who cannot sing. Although their father can make music happen, he does not have the strength of character to sing. Bullet, Liza's youngest brother, was unable to carry a tune. Too consumed by hatred and anger for his father, who built walls rather than music, Bullet would not or could not reach out of himself and was thus destroyed.

Seventeen Against the Dealer (1989)

In *Seventeen Against the Dealer*, the last book of the Tillerman series, Dicey has tried a year at college but finds this conventional road to financial independence lacking. She wants to support herself by building sailboats. To Dicey, building sailboats is a metaphor for a balance between responsibility and independence. Before she arrived at Crisfield, Dicey had her first experience sailing: "Boat, waves, water and wind: through the wood she felt them working for her. She was not directing, but accompanying them, turning them to her use. . . . It wasn't power she felt, guiding the tiller, but purpose" (*Homecoming*, 201). As her name implies, she belongs to a family whose lives are ultimately guided more by inner motivation than the external powers of conventional society; the Tillermans are individuals who map their routes adjusting their sails to what they feel is needed for their family. Now she is an adult, and her sister and brothers seem safe. James is a student at Yale, Sammy and Maybeth are in high school with friends and activities of their own, and Gram seems to be getting along without her. So Dicey throws herself into developing a business, making her own paths without signs. Metaphorically, she learns the risks of sailing without a chart, discovering by painful experience the need for insurance, written contracts, and financial savvy. Her ignorance about common business practices leads to her financial failure, as does her misplaced trust in the drifter Cisco Kidd, who may, unbeknownst to Dicey, be her father. He asks a lot of curious questions and then absconds with the money that he may feel is rightly his.[5]

So involved does she become in the quagmire of business that she almost forgets to hold on to her family and to Jeff, whom she has promised to marry. At the end, she finds that the cycle of reaching out, holding on, and letting go is never completed: "She wasn't finished learning," and she would not be until, in Gram's words, she was "older than dead" (196). Letting go is dangerous, "but never building [a sailboat], that would be a real failure" (198).

In *Homecoming*, Dicey learned to hold on, to keep her family together, to find a home and hold on to it. In *Dicey's Song*, Dicey and her family can afford to reach out, to learn how to trust and include others in their lives. By the time of *Seventeen Against the Dealer*, Dicey's family is strong enough to let her take the risk of letting go. Sammy keeps her from ignoring Maybeth, and Maybeth keeps Gram from succumbing to her own pride and illness. Dicey's family can now afford to give her "the chance to take a chance." And Dicey has "the eye to recognize it . . . the hand, to reach out and hold onto it. And the heart . . . or wherever courage came from" (209). With Jeff, who first reached out to her with song, and the larch wood she has had the courage to hold on to, she has the freedom to build a sailboat. "She'd probably make mistakes, but her mistakes would tell her what she needed to learn" (208). She can afford to do a little letting go.

Critical Perspectives

Critics almost universally praise Voigt's Tillerman novels, especially for their distinctive characterizations, even of the minor characters, which remain consistent throughout the series. Christine Behrman, writing in *School Library Journal*, represents the general consensus: "Voigt permits readers to know her characters in a way they rarely know people in real life."[6] Dicey and Gram are often singled out as particularly memorable.[7] Voigt is accused of stereotyping in *The Runner* and *Come a Stranger*;[8] however, these books merely portray in "meticulously authentic" detail the racism that existed in that part of the country in the 1960s. Voigt declares, "These are American books and it's part of American life. I raised a few questions about it. What do we really think? What would we really do?"[9] Her characterizations of African-Americans include a wide variety of individuals: the runner Tamer Shipp, who, though already married at twenty, plans to attend college, and succeeds; the French-born Patrice, who played a part in the French resistance movement against the Nazis; the kindly owner of the circus who protects Dicey and her siblings from an evil farmer; the intelligent natural leader, Mina; and a host of minor characters. Expressions of racism range from the honestly felt but mistaken opinions of Bullet, who has not experienced or thought about the implications of his prejudice, to the mean-spirited but artistically justified rationale of the mistress of the ballet camp for not retaining Mina after she has grown.

Voigt's characterizations are so inclusive that readers may recognize some uncomfortable realities of our society. In her *New York Times* review of *Homecoming*, Kathleen Leverich remarks on the "alarmingly hostile characterizations of most adults" (Leverich, 38), and this theme is reiterated in a review of *A Solitary*

Blue, where the mother, Melody, is seen as a "monster,"[10] an "appalling mother-philanthropist"[11] who steals Jeff's childhood by insisting on remaining irresponsible and self-centered.[12]

Voigt's children must become adults early, as they are abandoned either physically or emotionally by incompetent parents or threatened by selfish adults who place their own gain above their concern for children. Realistic fiction portrays the world as it really is for many children previously ignored in literature for young adults. Moreover, Voigt's gallery of adults includes an equal number of parents or surrogate parents who model intelligent concern and a talent for nurturance: Patrice in *The Runner* does more for Bullet than both of his parents; Brother Thomas in *A Solitary Blue* guides Jeff's father to show the care he really feels; Gram, determined to succeed with her second batch of charges, shows a depth of caring and a breadth of wisdom that any parent would envy. Most critics find Voigt's portrayals of both adults and children in the Tillerman series a realistic mixture of strengths and weaknesses, an intriguing blend of self-centeredness and self-denial.

Voigt has a strong sense of place; her settings, particularly the marshes and water scenes, offer comfort to the characters as they seek to develop inner strength. On the long trip to Bridgeport, Dicey takes the children from busy Route 1 toward the shore whenever they need rest and relief. Eight years later, while she is trying to build boats for a living, it is still the quiet rural roads and marshes that inspire Dicey's best thinking. When the characters must travel into urban settings, they are oppressed by the concrete, the trash, and the closed-in feelings of city life, whether it be New Haven, Bridgeport, Baltimore, or Annapolis.

Several critics see parallels to the mythic adventures of Odysseus in the first two books of the series.[13] James Henke, in a fairly lengthy analysis of *Homecoming,*[14] also finds numerous allusions in the plot to the fairy tale "Hansel and Gretel," the story that James tells his siblings as Dicey is trying to figure out a plan after her mother has abandoned them. *Dicey's Song,* which won the coveted Newbery Award in 1983, is generally recognized as more cohesive and fully realized than its predecessor,

Homecoming.[15] Both books are recommended as "classics" in a number of critical sources about young adult novels: *Seventeen Against the Dealer* was selected as a *Booklist* Young Adult Editors' Choice in 1989. *A Solitary Blue* is another favorite of critics, who appreciate the delicately precise portrait of Jeff's pain and the eventual realization of inner strength in both himself and his father.[16]

The length and complexity of some of the novels concerns some critics,[17] who feel that young adults who are only average readers may find the stories dull and difficult to read (Sutton, 40). Others chide Voigt for stretching readers' credulity in resolving her plots[18] or using her characters to preach her views.[19] Yet these criticisms are tempered with recognition of how Voigt's digressions and surprises add to the thought-provoking nature of her books. In her Newbery acceptance speech, Voigt describes a "stunning book" as one that "engages the imagination, sets to work the intelligence, and fills the spirit" (Voigt, *Horn Book*, 404). The Tillerman books are complicated and full of hard facts of life, but they fill the spirit with the wisdom and courage of their characters.

4. Learning to Live: Ways of Knowing[1]

For Cynthia Voigt, the key to defining an independent self is the ability to learn, to develop strengths and to gain adequate knowledge about the context in which a person lives. The ability and the patience and the chance to know what choices are possible are prerequisites for constructing an individual identity strong and capable enough to survive and support partnership with other human beings. Voigt believes that this maturity is important not just for relationships between males and females but for relationships between young adults and their families, and even for the relationship of young people to their emerging selves. Individuals cannot be autonomous and authentic until they consolidate their own identities, accepting their limitations and working toward dreams appropriate to their strengths, and the catalyst for this is learning. Coming to know oneself, especially in relationship to one's world and to others, is a major theme in the novels following the Tillerman series.

Women's Ways of Knowing is a study of women in society that can provide some insights about Voigt's characters. In this book, the authors posit five ways that women (and perhaps also men) learn:

1. Silence: a position in which women experience themselves as mindless and voiceless and subject to the whims of external authority;
2. Received knowledge: a perspective from which women conceive themselves as capable of receiving, even reproducing, knowledge from the all-knowing external authorities but not capable of creating knowledge on their own;

3. Subjective knowledge: a perspective from which truth and knowledge are conceived of as personal, private, and subjectively known or intuited;
4. Procedural knowledge: a position in which women are invested in learning and applying objective procedures for obtaining and communicating knowledge;
5. Constructed knowledge: a position in which women view all knowledge as contextual, experience themselves as creators of knowledge, and value both subjective and objective strategies for knowing.[2]

Although the title of this study by Mary Field Belenky and her cohorts indicates that these are steps in the ways that women learn, all of Voigt's main characters can be said to pass through these steps in their quest to form workable identities and solve the dilemmas that block this quest. Her protagonists begin as obedient and uncritical, silent or inarticulate about their own reactions to life and people around them. A major step toward growth is their realization that they can express opinions and ideas that are different from the expectations or conventions of the context in which they live. Although these ideas are often adopted wholesale from another authority, this first experience of assertion is essential to the process of defining a separate identity. Voigt describes this first step in her novel about a "nice girl" who inadvertently becomes unconventional.

Izzy, Willy-Nilly (1986)

In *Izzy, Willy-Nilly*, Isobel ("Izzy") Lingard, a pretty fifteen-year-old cheerleader, enjoys high school and concerns herself with popularity, prettiness, and parties. Like Ann at the beginning of *Tell Me If the Lovers Are Losers*, she is content to live according to the upper-middle-class values of her family and friends and does not spend much time reflecting on them. When she is invited to a party by a senior, Marco, she gladly accepts because she hopes to attract the attention of Tony Marcel, the boy she really admires. On the way home from the party, Marco, drunk from too many beers, passes out and they crash into an elm. When Izzy awakes in the hospital, she has lost part of one leg and is now "crippled." To please her parents and to appease her friends, she acts like the "nice girl" she is, cheerful and brave. She acts according to the knowledge she has "received" from her family.

But inside, she has a vision of a miniature Izzy, a doll-like creature that mirrors her subjective emotions, the grief and sorrow she really feels, and also the anger and hurt. She keeps these separate, trying to please her friends and family by appearing as normal as possible during the day but weeping at night, privately. Her public self goes through the motions of acquiescing to the steps of recovery, while her inner self, kept private, rebels and expresses her anger and her fear of the stares she will inevitably receive when she returns to school.

While she recovers, Rosamunde, unpopular in high school because of her forthright intelligence and her different values, imposes her friendship on Izzy. She shocks Izzy and her mother with her practical realism. But her probing questions force Isobel to reflect on her situation, the refusal of her friends to accept her as part of their group now that she is physically different, and the narrowness of her family's values. Before her accident, Izzy had been content with her superficial knowledge of her world and the people around her; now she is willing to see beneath the surfaces. Her friendship with Rosamunde has given her the courage to face reality and search for viable solutions. "You're a good person to be around, you know?" she tells Rosamunde. "You sort of make me think about things and get me doing things. I was pretty stupid, I think, about people, before—"[3] "Well, experience broadens us—or what's the good of it, right?" answers her new friend, expressing Voigt's conviction that reflecting and knowing about life is vital to personal growth.

With Rosamunde's help, Izzy has the courage to face the new experiences of being different in school, a girl on crutches without a leg. Now Izzy reflects on the deeper meaning of people's responses to her and reacts authentically, knowing them as they are beneath their social veneer, and relishing their reactions. In this novel, Voigt is reiterating the theme of her early books, where characters come to know themselves by moving beyond their first impressions and self-centered subjective impressions and reaching out toward new experiences to learn more about themselves and their world. Like Mina's in *Come a Stranger*, Izzy's first experiences in accepting the limitations of having a body different from our society's ideal are painful but ultimately lead to a recognition of her more important strengths.

This is one of the few novels for young adults in which the disabled person tells the story,[4] yet it is less "a book about learning to live without a leg . . . [than] a book about a girl learning to live."[5] While some critics think this book too long and over-explained,[6] others praise it for its perceptive characterizations of a middle-class environment.[7]

In Voigt's novels, children are often more capable than the adults around them because they are willing to expend more effort and imagination in trying to find solutions to life's obstacles and less likely to accept the status quo. In *Building Blocks* (1984) and in *Tree by Leaf* (1988) the young protagonists rescue their families from an overwhelming passivity. They question the knowledge received from authoritarian figures like parents and interpret its validity according to their subjective experience.

Building Blocks (1984)

Building Blocks opens with a typical argument between seven-year-old Brann's outspoken energetic mother and the quiet, rather passive father he despises. His mother wants to sell a farm they have recently inherited to pay her tuition at the law school where she has been accepted. His father refuses, blaming their financial problems on fate. Disgusted at his passivity, Brann asks, "What does that mean, it's fate?" His father mumbles a response: "Fate? It's what has to happen and you can't fight it."[8]

Exhausted by his father's hopelessness, Brann wanders into the basement workshop and crawls into a fortress built of oak blocks, handed down from his father's own childhood. Brann falls into a deep sleep, and when he awakens he finds himself in the room of Kevin, an overly responsible, undersized boy that turns out to be his father as a boy. Kevin is the oldest son of a construction worker, made gruff and harsh by his experiences staving off poverty in the Depression of the 1930s. As Brann, now trapped in the past, follows this boy who will become his father, he begins to understand why his father is so timid and cautious; every mistake Kevin makes is harshly castigated; he receives the blame for all the faults of his sisters and brothers from parents too overworked and fearful to be gentle. But Brann is still impatient with his father's passive acceptance of his situation. When Kevin will not or cannot stop his twin siblings from torturing frogs, Kevin defends himself: "It's fate." "Fate, my left foot," Brann says (43). He knew he was angry in the same way his mother was when his father used that expression.

In an effort to elicit some sense of adventure from his father, Brann rashly convinces Kevin to explore an underground cave, promising him respect and friendship. When Brann becomes hopelessly lost, he thinks about the nature of his plight and tries to fathom the best response to life: "It's fate. And you had to grab fate if you were worth anything. 'That's the hard truth,' he said to himself, 'you hear?' If you have to grab fate then you grab it, like Arthur grabbed Excalibur to take the sword out of the stone. Because he must have grabbed Excalibur the same way, at the end, to throw it back into the water, the hilt hard and heavy in his hand, and both of them were fate" (68). This thought keeps him brave, but he cannot find an exit until Kevin uses his spatial imagination to retrace their steps. It is Kevin's caution and his thoughtful attention to detail that save them.

Brann begins to see the value of these traits in his father. When he finally returns to his present-day life, he thinks about how his family can solve their dilemma. Realizing that his father's drawings might have monetary value that would allow his mother to follow her dream of graduate school, he convinces his father to suggest a compromise to his mother. Brann suggests, "Tell her it's fate": "'Fate isn't what either of us thought it was,' Brann says to himself, the idea going off inside of him like a sparkler.

Fate wasn't a smothering pillow, and it wasn't a steel sword blade. Fate was possibilities, all the possibilities, even the impossible ones" (120). This compromise will allow his mother to attend law school and his father to retain the farm he had loved so dearly as a child.

How does Brann become so wise about his family's fate and the possibilities that might exist? Perhaps Brann's journey to his father's boyhood is a metaphor for his willingness to imagine the reasons for his father's passivity, a loving desire to understand the man whose weakness threatens his own sense of family security. This "smooth blending of realism and fantasy"[9] create a changed relationship between father and son that is "both touching and believable."[10] Voigt explores the same mysterious access to seeing and understanding in *Tree by Leaf*.

Tree by Leaf (1988)

Set in rural Maine right after World War I, *Tree by Leaf* tells the story of Clothilde, age thirteen, discouraged by the changes in her mother when her handsome father, Benjamin Speer, returns from World War I with his face horribly disfigured by a war injury. The son of a wealthy manufacturer of electric carriages, he had married a Catholic orphan and been dismissed from Yale. His father has allowed the family to live with them but treated them like social outcasts. When Benjamin decided to join the cavalry, taking his magnificent horse, Bucephalus, his wife and children had been banished to Speer Point in Maine, an old estate that had been deeded to Clothilde by an aunt of the same name. During the first years of war, his wife had managed the farm with hard work, living on garden produce and mussels and clams gathered from the sea. However, now Benjamin has returned. Broken in spirit and ashamed of his disfiguration, he hides in the old boathouse and lives like an animal, not eating the food they bring him or keeping clean. Clothilde's mother has stopped performing the daily chores, playing the role of a lady of leisure, leaving the responsibilities of raising her youngest daughter,

Deirdre, and managing the household to Clothilde and their servant, Lou. Nate, Clothilde's older brother, abdicates his responsibility, running off to his wealthy grandfather, who has offered to raise him as a gentleman and heir to the factory his father has refused to inherit. Distraught and confused about how to manage this sudden responsibility, Clothilde hears a Voice, a Voice whom she thinks may be God. It seems to inform her that Nate will not go off on a cruise with his friends, that Lou will be able to escape from her father, who hits her when he has been drinking, and that Speer Point is not hers. After her encounter with this mysterious Voice, Clothilde is able to see the land around her with amazing clarity. She sees each leaf in detail and understands that, as the leaf grows, so grows the tree.

The next day, a thick fog envelops the land. Lou's father is lost at sea; Lou has escaped her father's abuse but at a cost that horrifies Clothilde. She finds that Nate has used the excuse of a cruise to escape to their grandfather's house, and that her parents are thinking of selling Speer Point to support them. With her new clarity of vision, she begins to understand the adults around her. She discovers that her mother has ceased to manage the household in order to play the part of the gentlewoman that she thinks her husband will love again. And she discovers that her father has considerable artistic talent that can be marketed.

In understanding the truths of their situation and facing reality as it is, the family succeeds beyond any of their wildest dreams. Clothilde's ability to reflect deeply on the nature of people and the possibilities in their situations eventually enables her to become a renowned psychologist; the family sells the lumber from the land to finance her education. She sees that her sister's greed is a need for affection and is able to guide her toward a more satisfactory life, a life in which she breeds dogs that satisfy her need for undivided affection. Eventually Clothilde bequeaths the land to a young relative she has only met once, but whom she has perceived has the same stubborn independence as herself.

The descriptions of this novel's setting evoke the mystical quality of Clothilde's search for control in her life;[11] "the solid landscape forms the base above which the story drifts like a fog."[12]

The stilted language of the dialogue reflects the sharply delineated roles assigned to people according to their social class and gender, yet the novel depicts the personal struggles of the main characters against the sudden loss of income and status in a way that is thoroughly relevant in modern times. A complex, thought-provoking novel, this is "for those [teenagers] who question the 'why' of difficult situations or seek a reality beyond surface circumstances."[13]

In this novel, Voigt's young hero seems to develop insight beyond the adults in her life by the same kind of magic that enabled Brann to understand the motivations of his father and mother. This insight seems to be "received" from some supernatural force; it is knowledge that enables her to see but not always to understand. Both Brann and Clothilde question the knowledge they "receive" and, finding it inadequate, invent their own personal explanations. For them as for other subjective knowers, "Truth is no longer conceived as absolute and singular but multiple and infinite" (Belenky et al., 62–63). Clothilde and Brann look for alternate answers and find solutions where the whole family can work together in a partnership that supports the dreams of all the members.

Voigt honors two kinds of knowledge—both the "instinctual" knowledge of people that comes from paying attention to relationships and the intellectual knowledge that comes from studying the written word. Generally, knowledge of people, called "instinctual" because its logic has not been articulated, is either "received" or subjective. When the source of this knowledge is family or social tradition, it is validated by the authority of these institutions. When individuals question the validity of this authority, they begin to rely on their own experiences and observations to validate their ideas. To the degree that each person's experience is limited, this kind of knowledge is narrow and often inadequate in new situations. Procedural knowledge, which includes academic knowledge, widens personal experience, providing a range of vicarious experiences and authoritarian interpretations. For Voigt (as well as Belenky et al.), using scholarly procedures to extend and deepen personal experiences and prejudices is the key to becoming an independent authority, able to construct one's own values and to create one's own interpretations of experience.

But academic knowledge without personal experience can also be used as a wall that blocks and limits; Bullet's father lived this way and destroyed his family and his farm. On the other hand, Dicey failed in business because she failed to follow procedures to learn about the world beyond her personal experience. For Voigt, individuals grow as they learn to balance and apply "intuitive" knowledge of people and the social rules they create with the "intellectual" apprehension of information and skills that enable accomplishment and conversation in the social world.

The Vandemark Mummy (1991)

In *The Vandemark Mummy*, the mystery is solved and a life is saved by both the experiential or subjective knowledge of Phineas Hall and the procedural scholarship of his sister, Althea. Phineas, twelve, and Althea, fifteen, arrive in a college town in Maine with their professor father, who has finally received a position where he can teach in his own field. Phineas is socially adept, an attractive young man who makes friends easily. Althea, shyer, following her father's footsteps, studies classical Greek as well as other ancient mythologies that define "Western culture," preferring to read rather than to mix with others. Their mother has taken a prestigious position working for a congressman on the other side of the country in Portland, Oregon. They are barely settled into their routine when a collection of Egyptian artifacts arrives, including a mummy with a lovely face painted on the wrappings and some sort of writing visible on the feet.

Professor Hall is put in charge of the collection, much to the chagrin of his colleague, the ambitious Dr. Simard, called "Rugman" by his students. Ken Simard hangs around, helping with the unwrapping and volunteering background information, especially when the press is around. When Althea notes that the writing on the mummy's feet looks like Greek, perhaps poetry, this self-avowed expert undermines her suggestion, asserting the authority of his maturity and his formal education. When the mummy is kidnapped and her feet smashed, it is the unquestioning trust of Simard's authority that keeps anyone from imagining what turns out to be the truth, and it is Althea's trust in Dr. Simard's character as a scholar that prevents her from seeing him as a dangerous criminal. The minds of Althea and the others are thus silenced by Dr. Simard's apparent authority.

When Althea starts to trust her own observations and experiences, informed by her study of Greek poetry and her knowledge of scholarship, she solves the mystery. But, thinking like a scholar about unknotting the truth, she forgets to consider how Simard the person might react to her suspicions and foolishly confronts him alone with her solution. "That was dumb. Because it *was* a criminal case. I thought [the mystery] out, but I wasn't thinking [about the crime]."[14] The scholarly Althea leaves a message to her brother in a code, although there is no practical reason not to communicate directly. This academic impulse also puts her in danger.

In contrast to his sister, Phineas is efficient and straightforward, relying on his experience with people to form his judgments. However, his mistrust of his own abilities to understand keep him from recognizing the importance of his own comprehension. "I'm just a kid," he says again and again. But his mind registers more than he admits. After a day of struggling to figure out where Althea has disappeared to, he wakes up in the middle of the night: "he knew where he might find Althea. He didn't know how he knew . . . , didn't care where the idea had come from" (161). When he is outside the library, he uses his knowledge about himself and his usual habits of thinking to carefully systematize his search; his persistence pays off and he finds his sister.

Some critics find this mystery disappointingly "less ambitious . . . a small[er] story"[15] than Voigt's usual work; others consider the lack of a neatly tied resolution to the family separation nicely realistic.[16] The feminist issues surrounding Mrs. Hall's decision to accept a prestigious position away from her family and the ensuing anguish underlie the neatly plotted mystery and help elucidate the personalities of Althea and Phineas, who both defend themselves from further hurt: Althea by burying herself in scholarship and Phineas by brazenly denying any sensitivity. This novel intertwines the logical puzzle of the mystery with the emotional impact of family separation to create a tension that mirrors the ways her two protagonists approach the problems in their lives.

Voigt gives credibility and value to both the instinctual type of thinking, which seems magical and illogical because it is based on unarticulated observations, and the more consciously logical, systematic study of a situation. Both Phineas and Althea are successful because they finally construct new ideas by admitting the authority of both types of knowledge. In this sense, *The Vandemark Mummy* harkens back to Voigt's earliest novels, where Ann in *Tell Me If the Lovers Are Losers* and Jean in *The Callender Papers* use both types of knowledge to learn from their new experiences and to define their identities, finally learning to trust the impulses of their hearts along with the clarity of their minds.

5. Heroic Ventures

Voigt's trilogy of historical romances, *Jackaroo, On Fortune's Wheel,* and *The Wings of a Falcon,* are written in the traditional heroic manner. Gwyn plays the "swashbuckling female,"[1] in a fast-paced tale of a well-meaning young girl who rides as Jackaroo to help the poor. Birle mixes her fortune with that of her romantic ideal, the handsome prince Orien, until she too attains royal status and power. Griff and Oriel escape from absolute tyranny and brutal conditions and finally become contenders for the title of Earl. In all three, the protagonists stride out to shape their destinies, seeking power in a world where most are disempowered and encountering life-threatening dangers with courage and intelligence. In their quest for heroic power, each is supported by a loyal friend who shares their adventures and helps further their quest for power. It is the faithful devotion of these companions that mitigates the accidents of fortune's wheel and provides a source of wisdom, advice, and comfort. Voigt's protagonists mature as they recognize the limitations of seeking power alone and learn the value of sharing their lives with others.

These three interrelated novels are set in a medieval feudal era before photography, painting, and even writing could record the daily events and scenery that shaped the development of our modern culture. Voigt writes from within the minds of her central characters, chronicling their reactions to the events and people they meet and examining the formation of their motivations; the reader vicariously feels their fear, knows their discomforts, and realizes the extent of their courage and commitment to their friends. The history Voigt has imagined occurs in a northern European land bounded by snowy mountains and deep forests with rocky harbors toward the south. The language sounds Scandinavian, more like Old English than modern German, and the people value obedience, justice, and hard work. Most are peasants who eat the turnips, onions, and potatoes they grow in summer, the meat and milk of goats, and the fish they catch in the rivers flowing from the mountains into their valleys. They dress in hooded clothes of woven wool and leather, unless they are gentlefolk, who sometimes dress in silk. Voigt vividly depicts the "limited diet, the limited worldview, the chasm between lords and common folk [as well as] the joyful release of a feast day."[2] Voigt's heroes in this medieval world, having discovered an escape from the routines dictated by their social environment, practice extraordinary courage and intelligence to win the right to make their own choices. In each case, the protagonist hero finds that his or her destiny is linked to the generosity of a deeply loyal friend who shares the risks as well as the excitement of the hero's path toward a life of greater freedom.

The people in the Kingdom, where this trilogy begins, are governed by a monarch who names two earls. Hildebrand rules the foothills at the northern border of the kingdom under the sign of the Bear, and the Earl of Sutherland the southern forests under the sign of the Falcon. Each earl is served by three lords whose bailiffs collect tithes and taxes to support the soldiers who keep the forests free of thieves and marauders.

Jackaroo (1985)

This novel begins at a time when food is scarce and the forests are unsafe. Several sons vie for the title of the Earl of Sutherland, and his lords and their bailiffs have become unruly and greedy because of the confusion that surrounds their leader. Every fortnight the peasants wait like cattle in the Doling Room to receive a basket of food to keep them alive during the winter. Ashamed and angered by the cloak of fear in which the other women huddle, Gwyn, the

Innkeeper's daughter, tries to alleviate that fear by helping those less fortunate. "Evil would be done, that was the nature of the world; that was bearable if good could also be done."[3] Though her first efforts seem discouragingly ineffectual, fate soon gives her the means to practice a more dramatic heroism.

When she and Burl, her father's servant, are asked to lead a lordly map-maker and his young son away from the village to survey the outlying lands, they are separated by a winter storm. Snowbound in a remote cottage, she cares for the young Lordling Gaderian, and he, bored into breaking the conventions that keep a lord from talking to his people except to announce and to order, reveals his identity: his father is Earl of Sutherland and he is heir to the title. Gaderian and Gwyn trade stories about their families and customs, teaching each other about the differences between the lords and the common people. He also teaches her to read and write, illicit skills for a commoner. While cleaning out a closet of the cottage, Gwyn finds the blue silk costume, the high leather boots, and the plumed hat and mask of the mythical Jackaroo, a secret she keeps to herself. This legendary outlaw, who like Robin Hood challenged the rich and the powerful and promoted the cause of the poor, avoided capture by using the mask, the costume, and the loyalty of the people, honoring the hero who gave them hope and self-respect. "Jackaroo could fight as a trained soldier. . . . He could ride a horse like a Lord: and he had the knowledge of letters which only the Lords held" (26). The rumors had some seed of truth, and this knowledge gives Gwyn courage.

When Gwyn and the Lordling return to the inn, she runs ahead to greet her family. She has cared for Gaderian well, keeping him warm and fed and soothing his terrifying nightmares, but now he is not with her, still playing the game of hide-and-seek the two had started on the long walk back. Assuming that his heir has come to harm, the Earl of Sutherland draws his sword and holds it to Gwyn's throat. Fear silences her and also her parents, who do nothing to save her from certain death. Only Burl speaks up on her behalf, just as Gaderian runs from his hiding place, turning his father's threat into apology. But Gwyn has learned how alone and vulnerable she is; her family has failed to come to her rescue, and she discounts the intervention of Burl, who is only a servant. The lord rewards both her and Burl for their services with purses of twenty gold coins and a promise of his loyalty, but this boon does not assuage her bitterness. Even more than before, she feels estranged from the social conventions that allow the rich lords to oppress the commoners. She decides that she will wear a mask of obedience and compliance, but will not submit in spirit. Soon after, when her father refuses to help the Fiddler, who is too poor to pay the newly established tax, Gwyn returns secretly to the cabin and, donning the costume of Jackaroo, walks out to the Fiddler's cabin and gives him one of her coins. The deed gives her the pleasure of seeing his relief and of hearing him tell the story of Jackaroo's generosity at the inn.

At the annual spring fair, Gwyn feels that she alone notices the misery underlying the celebration and questions the injustices of her feudal society. Seeing the body of a man hanged for his quick temper, she decides that "if there was one of these young men who also saw the hanged man, then that one she might take" (181). But she does not hear any man speak of it. She tells her father to announce at the fair that she will not marry, preferring the difficult life of a single woman to the subordination of her work to a husband.

Again she rides as Jackaroo, donating another of her coins to the poverty-stricken Am and then rescuing and delivering an orphaned infant to her sister who grieves the death of her first son. Dressed up as Jackaroo, she feels powerful: "in the disguise, she was free to do what she really wanted to do, much freer than was Gwyn, the Innkeeper's daughter" (196). When her father offers her a chance to reconsider marriage, she refuses: "She had made her choice and would abide by it. She had put on Jackaroo's mask and worn his clothes. She had become him and he had become her. . . . Others might try to impose their ways on her, but now they could not move her any more than the winds" (216). Encouraged by the steel in her voice, her father offers to make her heir to the Inn, but she refuses this as well. She realizes, with a start, that in defying convention to name a daughter as heir, her father is indicating great respect for her abilities and character.

But even in the guise of Jackaroo, her strength is limited. When she gives Am gold to pay his taxes, his boasting at the tavern about his newfound wealth, enormously exaggerated, instigates a violent robbery. Gwyn still does not have the power to overturn injustice, "because ride as she might, all the days and nights of her life, she could never do all that might be done. The Kingdom was too large" (213).

Moreover, as she assumes the traditionally heroic qualities of the mask she wears, Gwyn is losing her own identity. What started as deeds of empathy and caring now turn to a desire for vengeance toward the three thieves who have robbed and killed defenseless villagers. She uses the power of Jackaroo's persona to force the earl's proud steward to find and punish these men, taking his ring as a pledge, promising to return it when the thieves have been brought to justice. When her Uncle Win, who had also ridden as Jackaroo and who was about to be hanged as an outlaw, warns her, "what changes putting on the mask had begun, I had myself finished" (233), she recognizes the truth for herself. Her life is no longer her own: "Jackaroo rode outside of the law and that was why the Lords wanted to take him. The law could not hold Jackaroo. He would do what he wanted and that made him an outlaw. She hadn't chosen that, she had only chosen to do what good she could, for the people. . . . She had not known what she was choosing" (234). It is too late to escape. The steward appears in public with the three thieves he has caught, hoping to catch the man who rides as Jackaroo as he fulfills his pledge. Gwyn, invisible to him in her usual female garb, returns the ring by tossing it to his feet from the crowd. Embarrassed and confused, the steward accuses Cam, who is standing near Gwyn and whose foolish, scornful smirk makes him appear guilty.

Shocked at her own growing boldness and at the consequences of her actions, which increasingly endanger the people around her, Gwyn nevertheless rides again as Jackaroo to rescue Cam, whom she had once admired but now sees as weak. Attacked by soldiers waiting to capture the rebellious Jackaroo, her leg is badly slashed and she barely manages to crawl to a hiding place. Again Burl, whose gentle demeanor and lowly status have made him invisible to her, rescues her as in several previous incidents in the novel. By taking on the romantic and proud role of Jackaroo, Gwyn has lost the chance to inherit the Inn and even her privileged role as Innkeeper's daughter.

Crippled by her injury and with no public identity nor viable social role, Gwyn tries to imagine ways to survive independently. Burl encourages her to use her mind: "You're not a foolish girl, Gwyn; you've got a good head, better than most. Use it" (268). Finally she is rescued by the timely appearance of the young lord, who, reading her written message, convinces his father to let her travel with Burl under royal protection. In gratitude for Burl's care during the snowstorm and the quiet loyalty he has demonstrated since, the earl presents him with a farm and his freedom. Burl offers to marry Gwyn and she, finally recognizing his kind concern for others and gentle strength, gratefully agrees. They will use their knowledge and skills to establish an inn Gwyn has already named The Falcon's Wing. "But," warns Burl, "there will be no more Jackarooing about for you, lass" (287), and she, realizing how close she had come to death and defeat, agrees.

In this novel, Voigt creates a character who does not like the choices her society offers her: "Her life did not belong to her. . . . Were she to wed, her life would belong to the man she married. Were she to say no, her labor would belong to Tad [her younger brother] at the Inn, and she would become the Innkeeper's unmarried daughter, until she was too cumbersome or too old to work there" (96). Gwyn takes on the costume of the male Jackaroo so she can have the power to make her own choice, a power usually available only to a man. Is she "too blatantly symbolic of feminism in an era when women were really downtrodden,"[4] or is she merely using what fate provides to try to improve the world? She finds that men, lords, and even the legendary Jackaroo serve others "within the turning of [fortune's] wheel" (249), which limits them in their choices. What suits Gwyn is not taking on another identity, nor flaunting her power from outside the law, nor living autonomously unfettered by family; what suits her is to fulfill her own identity in partnership with a man who is equally strong and independent, and equally caring too. What has made her heroic is her couragous attempt to care for others and her recognition, finally, of the quiet heroism of Burl, the servant who has continually supported her.

Few readers are likely "to be astonished at this late blooming love affair,"[5] for Burl has kept her secrets, guarded her steps, and shared her sympathies. He is, in fact, the man whom she imagined she could marry at the Spring Fair, for he too had noted the injustices underlying the superficial gaiety. It is the discretion and kindness of Burl and Gwyn to the Earl of Sutherland and his son, rather than Jackaroo's impetuous forays, that have earned them an Inn at the southern edge of the Kingdom, where both can live and work free from the rivalries of the lords and their bailiffs. Critics generally have reacted well to this novel, appreciating the spirited courage of Gwyn and the steady gentleness of Burl.

On Fortune's Wheel (1990)

A generation later, Birle, "feisty and free-spirited like her grandmother,"[6] Gwyn, serves at the Inn. But while Gwyn wanted power to ameliorate injustices toward the poor and scorned to give the power of her work to a husband, Birle has attempted to use marriage to escape work and the poverty of her own family. She has promised to marry Muir, a rough-mannered huntsman who called her pretty and proposed to her. While Gwyn seeks romantic adventures to empower her, Birle pursues the Cinderella fantasy of escaping through romantic love. Like Gwyn, Birle precipitously grabs the first opportunity fate offers; she follows an intruder who is stealing her father's boat. When she faces the thief for the first time in daylight and sees "his smile [light] up the morning as the rising sun does . . . , Birle thought she understood everything about her self that she had never understood before."[7] She is in love, and happy to follow this lordly stranger to wherever he will lead.

But Orien has no idea where he is going. The eldest son and heir of the present Earl of Sutherland, he is the grandson of Gaderian, who ruled conscientiously for the good of the people, a sensitivity garnered from his long talks with Gwyn during their snowbound time in the cottage. Since Gaderian has grown old and Orien's father has just been murdered, Orien is fleeing the kingdom because he fears the political unrest that will follow and because he knows that the land will be better served by his younger brother, Gladaegal, a stronger man than he and more suitable to protect the people.

With Birle, Orien travels down the river beyond the safety of the Kingdom to the seaport, where law is merely the whim of the strongest army. Birle's knowledge of the river and the woods guides the first part of their journey, and her experience with butchering enables her to kill a dog that attacks them. When a storm drives them past the port and rough waves hurl them onto a rocky beach surrounded by unsurmountable cliffs, they are trapped without food or water for eight days. Like Gwyn and Gaderian, who learned about each other when they were snowbound, Orien and Birle trade information about their respective lives, Birle explaining how the peasants survive and Orien the expectations of court life. Their exchange engenders a mutual respect for the complexity of living that underlies the customs of both peasant and lord. On the face of a rock cliff, Orien carves their names, misspelling Birle as Beryl and neglecting to finish the "n" on his own name, inadvertently providing a name for Voigt's next medieval hero in *The Wing's of a Falcon* and thus linking himself to a future Earl of Sutherland.

After eight days the two are rescued by slave traders. Now Orien looks nothing like a lord, the shipwreck having reduced him to a shaggy skeleton without any evidence of his birthright. As a young woman, Birle has more value to the pirates. Orien tries to argue them out of danger, but it is Birle's kindness to the giant Yul that saves them from further harm.

Birle and Yul have the good fortune to be sold to Joaquim, a scholar who cares more about recording his knowledge of herbs than about immediate power and authority, and who allows them to roam the city with relative freedom. Birle's ability to read and write, learned secretly and illicitly from her grandparents and originally feared by her as burdensome knowledge, now gives her access to useful information and thus the ability to survive. As Joaquim's amanuensis, she copies formulas and alchemy books to fulfill the orders of his brother, the all-powerful Corbel, and she catalogs herbs to preserve her master's knowledge. Though separated from her beloved Orien and enslaved, Birle finds the neverending toil a relief rather than a burden: "Work had the power to distract, and distraction eased her heart" (166); "Work was a way of forgetting" (170). As she becomes more adept at identifying the herbs and writing down her newfound knowledge, the girl who had run away from the endless cycle of work-filled days at the Inn now begins to enjoy "the pleasure of a task her hands had done, and done well" (173). She begins to take pride in her accomplishments, even if they are done at the behest of a master who owns her: "As she sat at the table, carefully forming the letters and the lines of words, she could feel her spirit grow quiet. Aye, and why shouldn't she be proud of the pages she had written so flawlessly" (184).

While she learns the worth of work, she loses the clarity of her romantic attachment to Orien, whose enslavement has not been easy on him. She sees him in the market, cowed and disheveled.

> The joy of seeing Orien was a pain as sharp and bright as a knife. How could he have allowed himself to become what she had seen? It was all luck, she knew, and she knew also that her own luck had been good. But that didn't ease her. She wished she could forget the slave she had seen, and remember only the young Lord she had followed. . . . Hadn't he, she asked herself angrily, run away rather than be what he must be? He ought to have stayed where he was, to be Earl. (173)

Not until she is in danger herself does she fully understand "how many such moments had bowed him down . . . [and that] it was a wonderful thing that he could still lift his head to smile at her, helpless across a crowd of people" (178). To survive and be able to make choices, not only are work and skill necessary, but also the courage that comes from having a loyal friend. Orien can survive his unlucky turn of "fortune's wheel" because he sustains the hope that Birle will be able to help him.

Against almost impossible odds, Orien escapes from the mines where he has been branded and starved, and appears in Joaquim's backyard. Meanwhile, Joaquim prepares to flee the city, which is being invaded by the father of Celinde, a ten-year-old princess whom Corbel, the city's ruler, has stolen to be his bride and to legitimize his reign. In the ensuing confusion, Birle and Yul escape to the forest with the nearly dead Orien, heading north, back toward the Kingdom on the other side of the mountains. But first they are captured by Damall, a showman who will figure prominently in Voigt's next tale of adventure. Damall agrees to allow Birle and Orien to continue their journey if the giant Yul will work for him until one of them returns with a ransom.

Birle settles with Orien in a secluded glade, where she nurses him back to health. During this idyllic time the gentle summer sustains them, and their isolation gives them the peace to know each other again. When Orien asks Birle to lie with him as wife, she reminds him of their social inequality. But he reverses the meaning of her words to imply that she has been the "superior" despite his noble status: "Aye, there is, and ever has been. You gave me your heart and I gave you nothing in return, so now I give you mine—and we are equal." Birle sees in him "the hunger she had learned to fear" from other men, "but it was also longing . . . and she was not surprised to find in herself a hunger that matched his" (240–41). They lie together as man and woman in a love that is mature because they are equally committed to each other and equally experienced in knowledge of the ways that life can be hard. Now Orien knows what it is to have one's work be owned by someone else, and Birle knows the pleasure of working with her mind.

When they finally reach the Kingdom, where Orien is recognized as the next Earl, Birle lives in luxury far beyond what she had ever dreamed about as a child. She enjoys material wealth and the love of her handsome lord, and awaits the birth of their child, but she is not content. She has no work. Birle explains her disquietude to the old earl and his lady: "Among the people, a man and his wife are both necessary to the well-being of the house. I can't change myself into a Lady . . . who live[s] apart, even wife from husband" (264–65). Reluctantly understanding her desire to choose how she and her child will spend their days, they grant her permission to leave the castle and provide her with a farm.

Birle leaves without telling Orien and establishes herself on the land with the help of only her stepmother, Nan, who still cannot understand Birle's desire for independence. Birle knows that she can work without a man's help and that she can think for herself. Yet, when her child is born, she wants to give her "from Orien, his way of doubting, to ask questions when everyone said something must be so" (278), a habit of questioning that is now her way too.

On Fortune's Wheel is a feminist romance, a feminist wish-fulfillment. At the outset Birle is rescued by a handsome prince from a stepmother who treats her like a servant and a father too distant and weak to care. She soon finds that even the handsome Orien cannot protect her from the harsher evils of the wider world. She must learn to rescue herself, not with physical beauty but with strength and skill and courage. In the end she has it all on her own terms. Birle, even more than Gwyn or Dicey, embodies the feminist who wants to do her own work as well as to love. Having outgrown her adolescent dreams of a life without labor, Birle has her own farm and the freedom to choose her own work. But this is also a romance where hero and heroine are reunited. Orien has followed her and wants to live with her, earning his living as a puppeteer, telling stories to the village-folk.

> Orien stood before her with their life in his hands to give her, and Birle—as contrary as Nan said—could only think of herself. What of her own life? What of her own work? . . . Must she give that up? Birle could have laughed at herself. She had gone beyond a place where the world could tell her *must*. Aye, and they both had. Whatever Orien's work, she would grow the herbs and prepare the medicines, she would be herself and his wife too, and the mother to Lyss and whatever other children they had. She would be each of these, in the same way that Orien would be each of his puppets. . . . Her life was in her own hands. (287)

Orien, a traditional hero figure, could not have survived without the knowledge and skill of Birle. Now, committed to a life that will allow both him and Birle to choose their own work, he gives up the power that is legally his because he knows his brother Gladaegal will rule with more skill. And loyal to the promise they have made to Yul, he has traveled back to the city below the Kingdom and bought him back from Damall.

Several critics praise this adventure for its drama and its realistic depiction of slavery's degradation.[8] But the critic Victor Watson believes that Dicey, for one, would not have the patience to drag though this lengthy saga, which hints at political unrest and war but never explains its causes.[9] Another critic, Roger Sutton, sees no virtue in Orien but his bellflower eyes: "Dicey would have drowned him."[10] But Voigt raises significant questions about the complexity of power, both personal and political, that she wants the reader to ponder rather than answer herself, and Orien is a real human being who is thoughtful enough to know that the privilege of political power is bought with terrible responsibilities; he knows that he himself does not have the personal strength to handle power well. Indeed, the third historical fantasy of this series focuses on the differences between power attained through fear and power maintained by mutual respect and cooperation. Heroes engender their reputation and power by practicing courage, but they earn lasting respect by demonstrating wisdom and respect for others as well.

The Wings of a Falcon (1993)

Orien has ransomed Yul from Damall for three beryl signets, each emblazoned with the falcon that signifies the house of Sutherland. Voigt's third novel of this loosely connected series implies that Damall bought a small island with two of the beryls and began a dynasty of his own, where he raises boys from childhood and, at maturity, sells them back to the slave market. By the time of *The Wings of a Falcon*, the sixth Damall is a sadistic tyrant who amuses himself by whipping the boys and hearing them scream. The protagonist of this novel arrives at the Damall's Island without even his name, knowing only "that this

man would know how to hurt him." His only power is to keep his
fear secret. The boy squares his shoulders and decides to be as
"strong as stone."[11] But he is afraid of the water and of the day
when, like all the other boys, he would be dropped from a boat to
swim back to shore if he could, or to drown if he could not.
Attracted by the determination of this young boy, Griff, another
of the Damall's boys, secretly teaches him to swim. The boy
becomes a favorite of the others because he laughs and does
everything the best: he runs the fastest, swims the farthest, and
is handiest with the boats. He becomes the Damall's favorite.
Nikol, jealous, tries to cross him whenever he can; he steals the
dagger that the Damall has given him. On the other hand, Griff
becomes his friend, bathing his wounds and teaching him what
he knows of the island's history. The boy, sensing the danger of
Nikol's jealousy, tries to protect Griff by keeping their friendship
a secret. When the Damall names this nameless boy to be the seventh Damall, making his heart swell with pride and hope, he does
not tell even Griff; when the Damall changes his mind and
promises to name Nikol, the boy hardens again: "His heart was a
stone fist" (33).

When Nikol accuses Griff of poisoning the stew that has made
them all sick, the sixth Damall asks the boy to decide if Nikol is
right in his accusation. This is a test, and the prize is the power
that has made his heart swell, beyond its usual stone center: "He
didn't like his choices. . . . If he denied his own belief in Griff,
then he would have purchased his right to rule the island by the
betrayal of the one person in the world he trusted. If he acted as
he believed, then he would lose his inheritance" (40). He chooses
to support Griff; Nikol attacks him, and the two fight to be
named the seventh Damall. Nikol loses, yet the seventh Damall
declines to kill him. He knows it is a mistake, but, just as he
hates the whipping boxes, he does not want to kill. He is not
afraid, "but what kind of a life was it when you had to kill somebody to keep the place that had been awarded to you? What kind
of a world was it where in order to be on top you had to push others under?" (80). In order to survive, he would have to see things
as they really are, clearly and coldly without the soft edges of

misplaced trust or hope. But, despite the harshness and distrust he has learned to associate with power, he chooses not to kill.

Choosing to give up his title rather than exercise the cruelty necessary to hold it, the seventh Damall sails from the island, taking only his friend Griff. He finds a cliff with the name Oriel on it and takes it for his own; the name Beryl, chiseled beside it, seems to portend some connection to the name, for he wears the Damall's last beryl in a band wound around his waist. Oriel and Griff sail to the mainland, where they find work together on a farm kept prosperous by the production of salt. There they are content, working together for two years and flirting with Tamara, the Saltweller's daughter. This peaceful life suddenly ends when the savage Wolfers swoop down on the farm. Oriel and Griff try to stave off the attackers, giving Tamara time to escape. Had the two, faster than the young girl, run without concern for her, they might have escaped capture. But when Orien expresses bitterness at his decision, Griff assures him that it was a better choice to save the girl and perhaps the people she warned, even at the expense of their own freedom. Oriel discovers "that he desired Griff's good opinion, and hoped to keep it. . . . Griff was like his own hand—and when Griff disagreed with him, Oriel felt as if his own hand, even while it obeyed his wishes, had desires of its own, or ideas of its own. It was like watching his own hand walk away free, on its five fingers, and knowing that he had kept it bound to his wrist to serve his own convenience. . . . He had used Griff ill. But he had saved Griff too" (219–20). Oriel is beginning to appreciate Griff, not just for his loyalty but for his moral wisdom.

The Wolfers are ruthless raiders, killing without hesitation for convenience and loot, showing scorn for any sign of cowardice. Remembering his earlier training, Oriel turns himself to ice, eventually winning the grudging respect of Rulgh, the Wolfer's captain. Oriel can keep himself ice "against the heat of fires, the heat of blood, the heat of fear and fighting" (226), but he worries about Griff. Rulgh must never know "how closely Oriel's strength was bound to Griff's needs" (227), for that would make them both vulnerable to the man who would cruelly probe that weak spot, just to exercise his power. Without Griff, Oriel might become a Wolfer; Oriel realizes that he could enjoy the "Wolfer way of blade and fist and fire" (243) if Griff did not remind him of a gentler way of life. Oriel admires the fearlessness of the Wolfers, their single-minded pursuit of their goal, and even their carelessness of comfort and of life. But the bond to Griff is stronger.

An avalanche on the mountain to the North toward the Kingdom provides their escape from the Wolfers. Suddenly, after a year, they are free again. They make their way to a small farm at the edge of the Kingdom, the home of a hospitable young woman named Beryl. She is the granddaughter of Orien, who has taught her to work the puppets he has made, and she recognizes the special strength of this young man who bears with him a beryl with the sign of the Falcon on it. After giving her heart to Oriel and taking him to her bed, she tells him the significance of the signet. Now that the Kingdom is searching for a new earl, this beryl seems a sign, just as did the name carved next to Oriel and just as does the name of the young woman. "It seemed to him that his destiny had always been waiting for him. . . . He need only to go boldly forward" (297) and seize the power. Oriel seems to be called forth into another heroic adventure, one that takes him away from Beryl, who has given him her heart.

The three of them devise a plan to present him before the king and have him sponsored as contestant for the hand of Merlis, daughter of the Earl of Sutherland, and for the title. The plan is successful until Oriel discovers that the tourney must result in the death of one contender. Griff suggests that without death, former contenders can become friends. "I cannot enter such a contest," decides Oriel. "You fear dying?" asks one of the lords. "No," Oriel answers, "I fear killing" (333). The young boy who turned his heart to stone to become the seventh Damall has learned to value companionship and life more than power. Griff's friendship, Tamara's devotion, and Beryl's love have given him real strength, tempering the fear that made him seem hard and cruel to those he dared not protect. Impressed by Oriel's courage, the king and lords reconsider the rule and change their minds. There will be no killing and the king will sponsor Oriel.

Oriel desires the heart of Merlis as well as her hand, but she scorns this stranger who might win power over them all. She has given her heart to Tintage, whose suffering under the heavy hand of his father, Yaegar, has made his heart tender. Caught up in the quest for the power of the earlship, Oriel seems to have forgotten how much he cared for Beryl, who turns out to be the real jewel of the kingdom. Saddened at Merlis's coldness, Oriel knows that "her perfect lover would win the prize, and then lay it at the lady's feet. He would give to her the governance of her lands, and of her own heart . . . even though he was the most worthy." And he realizes that he is *not* that perfect lover. "He would win her, he would take her, willing or no" (382). Although he will not kill, the competitiveness that has been fostered so long by fear is too strong. He must win, must gain the coveted title. And so he is named Earl of Sutherland by the king.

But as Merlis puts her hand into his, as she must do by law, Oriel sees the fear and anger in her face, "like a woman who looks upon her fate with Wolfers" (390). He has won the title, but he cannot bear to cause the same despair that he himself has finally escaped; he opens his mouth to "give her life into her own holding" (390). But in that instant, he is mortally stabbed in the back by Tintage. It is the desperate act of a man whose love is stronger than his courage. Oriel has time only to name Griff as his successor.

Devastated at the loss of his friend, Griff is unwilling to rule, afraid of the dangers Oriel seemed to face without fear, uncertain of the decisions Oriel seemed to make without hesitation. However, for the sake of Oriel and his memory, he forges ahead, seeking the other lords' advice and winning their respect for his own courage as well as for his loyalty to Oriel. Griff's belief in cooperative rule inspires him to set a new precedent in government: an advisory council who will rule by consensus. He wins the heart of Beryl, too, by caring for the child she carries, Oriel's child, for whom Griff will preserve the title. "And Griff was what Oriel had shown him how to be, and needed him to be, and saved his life to be. Like Beryl, who was his lady, Griff carried on his breast the medallion that marked the house of the Earls Sutherland" (467).

With the inordinate strength that mutual loyalty provides, this partnership of Oriel and Griff has won them freedom from tyranny and the power to begin a new kind of government.

The power of fear and courage is strong, but the power of partnership is often more effective. Gwyn tries to right the wrongs of her society alone in secret, but she discovers that her deeds increasingly implicate others in a web that grows more complicated with each deed; she can not succeed without the help of Burl and the earl. Orien sets off on a journey alone; if Birle had not insisted on accompanying him, he could never have survived. Oriel and Griff succeed because, understanding the motivations of the people they must serve, they are able to earn their respect and change the rules of power games to their own advantage. Voigt's heroes learn that success depends as much on mutual cooperation as on individual strength, and as much on loyalty as on courage.

In addition to their common geography and political history, these three novels are linked by patterns of imagery. Voigt alludes to the strength of trees in the three books to characterize her male heroes. In *Jackaroo*, to Gwyn, Burl feels "as sturdy and deeply rooted as a tree" (248). From these roots grows Birle, the hero of *On Fortune's Wheel*, who thinks that Orien moves "with the grace of a young tree in a high wind . . . , straight and strong as a tree" (35). In Voigt's third book of the series, while Oriel makes himself like stone to fight his fear, "Griff had the bending strength of a sapling" (7) and hair "the color of dry leaves in fall" (17).

The more dominant image is that of the beryl which signifies the rule of the Earl of Sutherland. In medieval lapidaries, the beryl protects against peril and defeat, quickening a man's intelligence; it also can be made into a potion that cures diseases of the eyes. The *Kyranides*, a compendium of medieval medical lore, advises that the beryl be engraved with a crow, a crab, and a cypress.[12] Voigt ennobles the crow by changing it into a falcon, and names the hero of her third book Griff, a name loosely related to the German word for "claw." In *Jackaroo*, the name "Burl," the servant who protects Gwyn and sees the truth behind her masks, refers to the strong and knotted part of wood as well as serving as a rough homonym for the jewel. His name is echoed in his granddaughter Birle, who protects Orien, the nominal Earl of Sutherland in *On Fortune's Wheel*. In *The Wings of a Falcon* the jewel itself is worn as an amulet by Oriel, and its name has been given to Beryl, the mother of Oriel's child, the future Earl of Sutherland. In all three books, Voigt gives the name to a character who acts both as a protector as well as a guide, providing clear vision along the path to independence.

When Oriel enters the tourney to win the title of earl, he gives the beryl signet to the king to present to the next Earl of Sutherland and promises the mother of his child to Griff. In all three novels, the tree signifies the endurance of the family line, even in the face of peril, and the image of the beryl belongs to the character who protects his or her partner from harm and insures that the house of Sutherland will continue. Voigt's subtle use of this imagery contrasts with the straightforward movement of the plot and the blunt language of her characters.

The language of Voigt's novels reflects the directness of medieval communication, when words were few and poetic politeness was reserved for the noble, but the moral conscientiousness of the characters is modern. Voigt's heroes judge the rightness of their decisions by standards of justice and fairness. Daring to challenge the status quo, they question the rightness of tradition and custom, striving for the freedom to make their own decisions. They believe in the inherent value of all individuals, regardless of gender, class, or economic level, and they show equal respect for the ideas and possibilities of all persons. Voigt's historical romances are modern in their sensitivity toward these questions of equity, while they realistically reflect the physical hardships and the emotional and intellectual constraints of pre-industrial life. In these fantasies of long ago, Voigt imagines heroes who have courage to question, intelligence to survive, and commitment to maintain loyalty to their friends in an age where most people, peasants and nobility alike, sustain themselves with passive obedience to a customary rut, safe and same. Voigt's heroes cannot change the inevitable turns of fortune's wheels, but they do succeed in modifying their direction.

6. Daring to Live Authentically

Voigt's four later novels for adults or older adolescents illustrate the great courage necessary for living authentically. To live wholly and honestly, to choose life rather than merely to exist, leaves one open to pain as well as to joy. A major theme of *David and Jonathan* is that choosing to be open includes acknowledging and suffering the guilt of humanity's evil as well as knowing and enjoying its goodness. In *Glass Mountain* Voigt explores how individuals hide their fear of being open with masks and false appearances. The hero of *Orfe* can lead her friends and listeners into joy, but she cannot dispel the world's pains for them; individuals must experience their own angers and anguish as well as their own loves. *When She Hollers* depicts one girl's struggle to choose life and to become wholly her own while being abused by her stepfather.

In all four novels, the successful protagonists, or heroes, find courage to face life honestly by reaching out to a relationship that strengthens them: Henry commits himself to helping Jonathan resist David's cynicism; Alexis asks Gregor for one weekend together; Enny and Orfe and the three Graces make music as an integral group; and Tish trusts Mr. Battle with her whole story, including her fear and her anger. Voigt is illustrating that individuals who live passionately are heroes, liberating themselves from the constraints of fear by reaching outside of their self-centered worlds to connect with other heroes in a mutually supportive relationship.

David and Jonathan (1992)

With its brooding tone and the philosophical character of its major characters, *David and Jonathan* might be called Voigt's *Hamlet*; it is a difficult and intense work that centers on the decision of Henry, the narrator, "to be or not to be." Henry Chapin Marr, fifteen years old in 1958 when this story begins, thinks of himself as rather plodding and repressed, cautious about living and loving. His mother and father, living in an inherited home on Cape Cod, are conventional blue-blooded New Englanders, quiet and refined. Although his father was a conscientious objector during World War II, Henry plans to become a soldier and tries to practice the stoicism he believes he will need. Jonathan Nafiche is his best friend. He is Jewish, with a mercurial mind and temperament, laughing and light where Henry is cautious and somber. Henry's house, hidden behind scrub pines, is quiet, barren of noise and color and clutter; the Nafiche home is above the family restaurant, full of talk and the stray people they collect. Mrs. Nafiche has "speaking eyes. . . . Her features were too heavy and irregular for beauty, her mouth too full, her eyebrows dark and uneven; and she was the most beautiful woman Henry had ever seen."[1] His own mother has the balanced features of the Chapins and is tall, thin, and tidy.

One of the "strays" that comes to live with the Nafiches is David, a dis⁺ nt cousin who miraculously survived the Nazi occupation, bu⁴ not without suffering great psychological damage. Now he is twenty; at fourteen, he had been found by an American patrol, weighing only sixty-six pounds. The Nafiche family will try to provide a refuge for David, who is still suicidal even after years of expensive therapy.

When Henry first meets David, he is fascinated by his physical beauty and the look in his eyes: "[David's] eyes darkened by hope, the face alight with it—Henry couldn't imagine what David had seen to give rise to such a feeling . . . and he couldn't understand his own response, a desire to be worth . . . the intensity of David's eyes. . . . David's hope-filled eyes made time measureless.

Henry stepped back" (80). That night Henry dreams of David and ejaculates. "Just briefly, he let himself remember—and his whole body grew warm, like water flowing over it, the water like fingers—before he made himself forget" (83). This fascination, manifested physically, along with other signs, makes Henry realize that he may be attracted more to males than to females, a type of love not easily admitted in the 1950s when this novel takes place. This and David's constant reminders of humanity's evil side, the human capacity for harming and hating and murdering, make Henry want to avoid David. David repulses Henry; he is always jabbing and poking into Henry's private world, asking questions that probe into uncomfortable thoughts, challenging Henry to act more courageously than he feels. When Henry bludgeons a cat in order to put it out of its misery after it has been fatally injured by David's careless driving, it is David who forces the connection between killing animals and Jews. Henry vomits, "as if he could rid himself of the whole experience, and David, too. As if he could rid himself of himself, and what he'd done . . . , he had always used to like himself" (103). David, along with the dream he has had about him, causes "the most ungovernable . . . passionate feeling he'd ever felt . . . , and except that it was Jon, Henry would have turned his back on anything to do with David" (120–21). However, if Henry wanted to see Jon, he had to see David too. "Anyone who made you have the kind of dream Henry had had about David, even if it was only once—that was creepy. . . . Then he had to remember that David was Jewish. . . . When Henry remembered, he felt so sorry for David it made him feel sick" (107).

However, Henry cannot leave Jon now. David's insistence on reminding them of humanity's capacity for evil is wearing Jon down, eroding his former ebullient optimism and love of life. David's presence makes the question of how to acknowledge human evil impossible to ignore. Like Jonathan and his family, Voigt is asking, "How can a Jew live in this world and remain a Jew?"—or, for that matter, "how can anyone who believes in the humanistic code of mutual respect reconcile the existence of such horrid torture?" But one night Henry becomes so tired of facing the questions David presses on him that he cancels his plans to visit David and Jon at the restaurant the next day. That night David is missing; he has rowed out into the ocean and killed himself. Henry has failed his friend Jon by avoiding him and avoiding the pain that is part of his life. He would rather not face his own guilt as a privileged citizen in a world where genocide occurs, nor his inability to befriend its victims, nor even his suspicions about his own sexuality.

In contrast, Jon grapples with his thoughts to try to define his own role in David's death and in the larger world. He feels responsible because he found himself incapable of giving David the unconditional love that he needed, the kind of love that Jon's all-merciful omnipotent god asked from him. Henry responds: "But Jon, . . . You can't try to be God without choosing death, as a human" (225). There must be a balance between recognizing and accepting the impulses that are culturally defined as sinful on the one hand and striving toward a God-like ideal on the other.

Jon remembers the scripture: "See, I have set before thee this day life and good, and death and evil. I call heaven and earth to record this day against you, that I have set before you life and death, blessing and cursing: Therefore choose life, that both thou and thy seed may live" (152). When you choose life, "you're choosing all the—terrible—things, the worst you can imagine. . . . But that's only part of it. You're also choosing to celebrate" (154). Living is recognizing and accepting the possibilities of both great love and great pain. But, because living wholly and authentically is the only way to affirm hope, to limit the damages, it is preferable to mere existence; for Voigt, it is the morally righteous answer to the questions posed above.

In 1967, twenty years after David's death, Captain Henry Marr, surgeon, moves along the beds in a military hospital in Vietnam. He spies Jonathan Nafiche, with severe head wounds. He has been a POW, cruelly tortured, but until the end he is able to show spirit and humor to his fellow inmates, inspiring them to live. It has been the memory of David and his survival of David that has gotten him through. Jon *has* chosen life, though he has come to learn that "choosing life is like choosing . . . to have your liver taken out daily by an unskilled eagle. Or perpetual crucifixion" (224). Choosing to participate as best one can in the struggle to provide all humans with the choice whether to live or die, to be good or evil, is all we as free humans can do, Voigt seems to imply.

Jon's persistence in loving and living has made him a hero. Now he faces an operation to remove a piece of shrapnel embedded in his brain. Henry agrees to undertake the difficult operation, although he dreads the choices he must make. In the end, Henry saves Jon's mind—but in the process severs the optic nerve. With the same courage that it had taken to kill the cat long ago, Henry has been able to limit the damage. Henry, still careful and constrained, will also choose to live his life, making choices that may be painful but that do "limit the damage." Admitting his love for Jon, he decides to go back to Boston to live and work, keeping "close but not too close" (248), not denying his love for Jon but not letting it get in the way of Jon's choices either.

This is an intellectually challenging novel, long, complex, and full of Talmudic references.[2] The intense examination of "adult-size ideas and concepts"[3] might be more suitable for college-age students than younger adolescents.[4] The "hell of the Holocaust is not overcome by individual goodness," and the characters "talk as if they think and read."[5] However the "healing and wisdom that such books promote" reward the patience and effort required (Campbell, 31).

Glass Mountain (1992)

In Shakespearean tragedies, "at the end, the world of the play is made better, even though the individual is . . . lost" (*Seventeen Against the Dealer*, 18). If *David and Jonathan* is Voigt's *Hamlet*, posing the question "To be or not to be?" and ending with a world that sees the truth more clearly, *Glass Mountain* (1991) is her *Twelfth Night*, in which she explores individuals' choices about their identity and tests the validity of those choices. "We are none of us what we seem . . . except for those of us who are exactly what we seem,"[6] thinks Gregor, the narrator and hero of this comedy of errors and misguided deception. In this romantic comedy, Voigt displays a previously hidden talent for humor to explore the extent to which superficial appearances attract romantic attention and the way in which it deepens into more sincere love. If we are initially attracted to the appearance of an individual, and the role he or she seems to play in society, will we love the real person underneath? How much of us is unique—and how much of who we are includes our social status? Like Voigt's first two novels, *Glass Mountain* is about that first step of establishing an identity separate from family expectations and social traditions, that first step of defining an individual self in the context of a society that tends to define people by the social roles they appear to play. Like Orien, the prince in *On Fortune's Wheel*, this novel's protagonist, Gregor, first attracts love by the very attributes of good breeding and noble manners that he is trying to hide and yet finds that he is still truly and wholly loved when he is demoted to servant status.

In this novel about how appearances reflect the social self, the self we have decided to present in society, Voigt uses clothes and jewelry to describe her characters and their relationship to each other. At thirty-three Gregor is on the prowl, stalking the dens of upper-crust Manhattan to find a suitable woman to marry, a woman who is "moneyed." It is Valentine's Day, but his prey, one woman with "entirely lovely" hair and another with emerald earrings that "swing in the light," elude him. What he does find is Alexis, lunching alone in an expensive restaurant, a little tipsy on champagne, and dressed in the clothes of "a tall, stylishly thin woman, most certainly a woman of experience" (13). Unfortunately Alexis is short and plump.

When Gregor pursues her, not out of interest—she seems too young and plain—but to protect her from the dangers of New York until the effects of the champagne wear off, he finds that she is twenty-nine, well-educated, and mentally mature. She is also an innocent, lacking not only experience with honest "real" relationships but also the courage to know her inner self. Skittish and suspicious of any man who might befriend her because of her wealth, she refuses to give her name or tell her story. However, as the afternoon progresses, she recognizes a certain honor in Gregor and gives him her address: "You're a prince, whoever you are, a prince in prince's clothing" (23).

Perhaps. However, in the next chapter, readers see Gregor in another role; he is a butler, "prematurely stuffy . . . and unoppressively avuncular" (31), a perfect stereotype. His employer is Mr. Theo Mondleigh, a cheerful ladies' man who is enjoying his youth. His father is after him to settle down and to marry "Pruny" Rawlings, the only daughter of a respectable and wealthy Connecticut family. "The Rawlings are serious gardeners . . . and Pruny is their prize begonia. Or prize potato, that's more like her," says Theo, who feels choked by his family's pressure to marry her (43). He is attracted to more glamorous types.

Gregor decides to pursue the awkward but obviously moneyed woman he has rescued. His goal is marriage rather than love. But he is becoming charmed by the complexity of her mind: "Alexis shook out her mind like some women shake out their hair, to display its bright tumbling qualities, to attract. . . . Most women are less reluctant to show you their breasts than their minds, and I may know why. Alexis had not such qualms of modesty" (99–100). Alexis enjoys her times with Gregor, but she cautions that there is a man, another commitment. They continue to spend time together anyway, happy with each other's company. Gregor does not know her full name, and she, of course, has no idea that he is a butler.

Meanwhile, Gregor's employer dates all kinds of women. "Mr. Theo's affiliation might have been Episcopalian, but his tastes were catholic" (67). There is the owner of the husky voice who calls him "Mr. Bear" and the ash-blonde Holly, a redhead, and a curly-haired brunette, Muffy who is fluffy (67)—all of this in between dutiful, dull weekends with Pruny, to please his family. Events come to a head on the first of April, appropriately called All Fool's Day here. Theo proposes to Pruny, Gregor to Alexis, and two minor characters, Theo's younger sister and a man she has known less than two weeks, get married.

If this were a mere romance, the lovers would live happily ever after the wedding. But this is romantic comedy. For Gregor, the comic catch is that Theo's "Pruny" turns out to be Alexis. When she sees him in his role as Theo's butler, she immediately assumes that Gregor has deceived her in order to ascend the social ladder. For Alexis and her family, it is unthinkable that she would consort with a servant. Alexis is trapped by her conventional family, and Gregor is trapped in his role of the butler. Plans for Theo's wedding to Alexis proceed.

However, after the wedding, Alexis decides that the love she feels for Gregor, the kind of love in which two people are able to communicate beyond the conventional niceties, is preferable to her marriage of convenience to Teddy Mondleigh. Courageously she returns to Gregor and asks him to stop pretending to be what he is not. She is willing to live his life, entering domestic service as his partner. "No," says Gregor. "It would be a waste of your mind, your abilities." They must start out as equals, she insists; "No more sham life. The real one for the two of us" (272).

If they are to start out with no pretense, Gregor must doff one more disguise. He takes Alexis to his home, a palatial manor outside of Pittsburgh and reveals his whole name. He is Gregory Reikel, the heir to a mining company with far more money than she or Theo has. He is indeed a prince, a hero who has dared to leave the safety of his home and learn to live in the world on his own terms. He has dared to take on a whole new social identity so that he can find someone who is not marrying *him* for his money, and he has found Alexis. But it is only because she too has dared to leave the safety of her conventional family and to risk marrying a man she loves despite his lower social status that he has not lost her. They are now equals—in courage as well as in social background—and will live happily ever after.

As in Shakespeare's *Twelfth Night*, where the final dissolution of the hero's disguise brings happiness to all, the other lovers in the novel are also reunited with their rightful partners. Even Theo is reunited with his mistress, who really does love her "Mr. Bear." But as in Shakespeare's play, this story leaves some questions unanswered. Would Alexis have been able to love Gregor if he had not been born into wealth and privilege? She is relieved to hear that, in fact, he is her social equal—perhaps even wealthier than she. Has Gregor been fair to Alexis in his double deception? He could have saved her and himself much pain if he had revealed his true identity before her marriage to Theo. Voigt seems to be implying that only after Alexis has renounced her loyalty to her parents and the conventions of her childhood is she worthy of "the prince." Perhaps only after Alexis has discovered the courage in herself to leave Theo and disappoint her parents' expectations can Gregor believe that she loves Gregor for himself. But does not Gregor's "self" include his moneyed background? *Glass Mountain* leaves the viewer with the same bittersweet view of love and humanity and the deceptions it employs as does *Twelfth Night*. For in *Glass Mountain*, there is also much falling in love with appearances, much play-acting and artifice.

Besides images of clothes and cosmetics, Voigt uses allusions to the arts—drama, music, and painting—as metaphors for the artifice that her characters use to present themselves to each other. Like an artist, Gregor has conceived his quest for a marriageable woman with careful consciousness. In the beginning of the novel, as he is ready to put his scheme into action, he cannot conceive how to include the picture of his family background: "No matter how I moved, I couldn't bring the third staircase into the portrait [of myself]. Degas might have brought all the background in by distorting the point of view, Rembrandt might have suggested it in the shadowy darkness behind the illuminated figure, but only Picasso in his cubist period could have painted the portrait truly" (1–2). Gregor imitates Picasso by presenting himself to Alexis in abstract images that are truthful but without shading or details, that portray the truth about who he is, not as embedded in a conventional context, but in the sum total of the pieces of him she sees. It is a truth that demands persistence and imagination to perceive.

At the showing of Jordan Bradshaw's paintings, where Gregor begins to appreciate the depth of Alexis's mind, the paintings they observe, though ordinary and traditional at first glance, contain an intensity and depth of color unusual in watercolors. And when he makes love to her, he finds a "Renaissance forehead" (226) beneath the hairdo and a Renoir or Titian body beneath the dumpy clothes. The plays they see together, the concerts they hear together, the paintings they appreciate together—these all elicit conversations that display their inner selves to each other and skirt the issues of business, wealth, and social status. Art lets them discover each other unencumbered by social symbols of identity.

The title of *Glass Mountain* is borrowed from a short story by Donald Barthelme that depicts a foolish hero who climbs an urban glass mountain with no help but from "plumber's friends," as he calls the rubber plungers that help him to adhere to the slick vertical surfaces. At the top he approaches "the symbol, with its layers of meaning, but when [he] touched it, it changed into only a beautiful princess,"[7] whom he throws down the mountain to his acquaintances. Gregor thinks he is pursuing aristocratic wealth, a woman with the manners and money that make her suitable for an upper-class marriage. But he finds a real woman instead. What Gregor really wants and needs is a woman's trust in the self that does not depend on symbols of wealth and power; and, in the end, Alexis offers that to him with great courage and sacrifice. They are both rewarded with a future in which their relationship is founded on trust of themselves as individuals as well as on their love for each other. They have both met the tests of "print[ing] their own personal currency"[8] and are then able to write their own mutual story.

Perhaps, as Alexis points out to Gregor after they watch a production of *Twelfth Night*, the audience accepts the deception of the female-male twins, Viola and Sebastian, because they "want the story" (*Glass Mountain*, 61); they want the romantic plot to conclude happily for all and the world to be in peace and harmony. Similarly, it seems that Alexis, sensing the true prince beneath Gregor's butler clothes, has asked him to spend a honeymoon-like weekend with her before she marries Theo because she too wanted their story to end as a romance.

In contrast to *David and Jonathan*, *Glass Mountain* has been characterized as "light romance at its best,"[9] "escapist romance, but without stereotypical characters or plot,"[10] "an amusing book with a cracked ending."[11] "Voigt's fanciful milieu is so air-tight that the issue of plausibility never intrudes."[12] This is a realistic fantasy that many high school students would enjoy,[13] especially those familiar with Shakespeare's *Twelfth Night* or with Manhattan high society.

Orfe (1992)

"At the end of *Twelfth Night*, when the duke finally falls in love with Viola, you wanted that to happen. . . . It was what would happen in a well-ordered universe, so you believe it. . . . The whole play argues that love is irrational. You can't rely on it."[14] The world of *Orfe* is anything but well ordered, and love is not to be relied upon. Despite the loss of two individuals, the world of the play (or, in this case, novel) *is* made better by the songs and lessons that remain. This novel has the larger scope of tragedy.

Compared to Voigt's previous novels, with their down-to-earth and pragmatic tone, *Orfe* is dreamy and mystical, conveying its themes through allusion and suggestion more than by direct example. Usually Voigt's characters are steeped in specific family contexts and live in vividly realistic places. Henry and Jonathan's Cape Cod is visible to readers, and the Manhattan of *Glass Mountain* is very specific, but Orfe and Enny seem to have no histories nor identifiable roots, and the novel's scenery is generic.

The plot is an amalgam of three stories: the myth of Orpheus and Eurydice (including the legendary relation of Orpheus to the three Graces), a modern saga of the rock-music world, and the fairy tale "The Frog Prince." What does this complicated combination mean? Voigt interweaves these stories to illustrate the range of emotion, experience, and perception about human nature possible for those who reach beyond self-centeredness. Daring to love unconditionally, to give experience total attention, and to live for the moment take the kind of courage and wisdom we recognize in myth and folk-tale; Voigt includes these allusions to evoke a deeper understanding of human development than her simple plot might otherwise communicate. "Never has Voigt's writing been more poetic and more deeply resonant," writes

Diane Roback in an early review.[15] The language of this novel is intricately patterned, using repetition and alliteration to mirror the mythic nature of the story, and the imagery of light and fire and darkness colors these shapes with a richness that even the most superficial reader appreciates.

The names of the main characters underscore the allusions to the Orphic myth. Orfe, an extraordinarily talented singer and writer of rock songs, is reminiscent of the ancient bard Orpheus, whose songs enchanted his followers into frenzied "cleansing of the soul . . . a communion with the Beyond" (Wind, 3). Although not divine himself, Orpheus was famed among both gods and humans for music that was irresistible. In Voigt's novel the young schoolgirl Orfe simply seems different; her classmates call her "The Creature from Outer Space" and shun her, except when she sings. Orfe does not want to be ordinary; she wants to be famous, composing and performing songs that everyone will recognize as universally true. Unconcerned with the conventional values of her schoolmates, she does not seem to care if her peers talk to her, nor does she follow the rules of their games. In fact, like her namesake, she uses her talent to transcend order. When the students divide into teams to play Red Rover, she starts to sing. Whenever she sings, the children follow her instead of the rules, and the game becomes chaos.

Enny, the narrator of the novel, seems to represent "anyone"—an ordinary soul for whom "it was enough just to get through every day"[16]—an ordinariness that contrasts with Orfe's ambition and charismatic appeal; or perhaps "Enny" alludes to the faithful servant Henry of the Grimms' "The Frog Prince." With carroty red curls, Orfe, though "only just barely not unattractive" (23), is described as the kind of person that made people want to look at her and keep on looking, whereas Enny is not described at all. There are hints to suggest that Enny may be black—she especially mourns the bodies of blacks who are buried in Vietnam—or maybe she is sympathetic to the plight of all victims. At any rate, in the beginning of the novel, Enny seems to be a social nonentity, a timid girl who does care about the approval of her peers, so much that she does anything they ask. She likes the order of mazes rather than the creativity of paper dolls, and she does not even think about what she would like to be in the future.

Bound by her timidity and her automatic respect for the rules, she is taunted to tears by a group of boys in her class who name horrible deeds of torture and hate, driving Enny to weep for the pain in the world. Orfe is frustrated by her passive acceptance— "You act as if you're nothing, some absolute nothing"—and defines her friend's specialness: "It's ordinary to be self-centered. . . . Maybe you're the one who's extraordinary" (16). Orfe routs the boys by vomiting on them, but soon they are back, as if Orfe were a mere fly. Angry that they seem to devalue her friend, Enny dares to be angry and it feels good. She hits Rab with her lunchbox and is banished to sit alone in the hall for the afternoon. Unrepentant, she sits alone feeling as if she has just set herself free. The boys soon cease to bother her.

Years latter, Enny, now in college, meets Orfe again, singing on the street. "The song floated like light, both particle and wave" (21). The music made Enny feel "embraced, empowered . . . enchanted, . . . exalted" (32). But Orfe is also performing with a hard-core music band, "Jack and the Jackets," and what draws the crowd is when Orfe vomits, responding to a litany of newpaper headlines, a list of the world horrors. "Current Events" is the title of the song, and "It makes me sick" is the chorus. When Jack sings the words, "he pushes the words into [her] stomach, they ride in the music" (35) and Orfe "can't help swallowing them, and feeling them" (37). When Orfe vomits, the audience feels released, satisfied, as if she has taken the pain of living in a hate-filled world into herself and then expelled it for them. Jack says the audience needs it, and Orfe complies.

Furious at this waste of talent and Orfe's submission to a crowd, Enny agrees to become her manager and help her form a band of her own. They hire three back-up players. First Enny finds Grace Phildon, a pudgy black single mother, pleasantly easygoing and agreeable. Orfe introduces Willie Grace, also black but aggressively defensive: "the corners of her mind and tongue as sharp as bones." Raygrace, who becomes a "grace" on the spot, changing his name to convince the others to accept him, is a "little apple of a guy" (53) and white, but willing to please and desperate to join.

Orfe may also be a symbol of love, in its fullest sense, including charity—like the nude figure of Aphrodite attended by the three Graces. These vulgarized down-home "Graces" are a comic parody of the mythical trio who adorn classical legend, and who were extensively allegorized as Beauty, Chastity, and Desire in Greek and Roman art. Beauty is the quality that initiates the process of love; Chastity (or true and committed affection) refines the love into something more conscious and demanding, and Desire (or Love) inspires the consummation of the process. In Orfe's band, Grace Phildon is the first "grace," lovely in her gentle motherliness; Willie Grace, with her acid tongue, chastises, keeping everyone honest and "up front." The third "grace," Raygrace, tracks down the band himself because of his desire to join. Willie Grace and Raygrace do end up living and loving together at the end of the novel, but the symbolism carried to this extreme seems farfetched. Voigt is toying with classical iconography, using it allusively and with a sense of humor rather than adopting it slavishly.

The mythical Orpheus, distraught after his lovely wife Eurydice dies from a serpent bite, follows her into Hades. Enchanting the gods of the underworld, he receives permission to lead Eurydice back to life under the condition that he resists looking back at her during the journey. Almost at the edge of the underworld, overcome by his desire and love for her, he looks back, and Eurydice returns to the world of the dead.

In Voigt's novel, Orfe falls in love with Yuri, dark-eyed, dark-haired, with curls that "hung like the tendrils of grape vines" (78). When Yuri meets Orfe, he is on drugs. But he recognizes her as someone "like a flame like fire to burn you clean" (66). Yuri immediately leaves the house where he has lived, full of drugs and drugged friends, and goes through detox.

Afterward, he gets a job, starts school, and cleans up his life before he approaches her again. Their relationship progresses slowly and carefully. But Orfe is gleaming with love, writing two kinds of songs. Some are for immediate performance, "foot-lifting,

hip-hinging, arm-pulling music, for dancing" (59), but the others
are songs that "told [her] what she should have known all along"
(82), which was the truth. These songs she calls "Yuri's Dreams,"
and these are the songs that eventually are recorded by her and
the Graces and make music history. At first worried about Orfe,
Enny realizes that Orfe "wasn't burning herself out or burning
herself up—she was on fire" (58).

Enny sees that Orfe is for Yuri and Yuri is for Orfe: they radi-
ate a loving heat that she "can still warm my hands at, if I close
my eyes and remember" (20) and she agrees to walk before them
at their wedding. After their vows comes a parade of people from
the house where Yuri used to live, bearing a cake. Enny sees a
"silver knife blade flash, saw a square of cake in Yuri's hands,
saw him eating" (97) before he disappears, his pupils expanded
and his eyes darkened. The frosting has been drugged, and Yuri
is led back to the house of spaced-out friends, who choose a pain-
less deathlike existence rather than life. Later that night, Orfe
follows him to the house, which is nasty with the odors and dope.
The air is thick and smoky; for Orfe and Enny, it is "like being
underwater, among the drowned" (117). Playing her music, trying every song she knows and even inventing new ones, she
almost has him. He is walking down the hall with girls "hanging
on to him . . . or hanging off one another, like a human chain"
and holding on to her hand. But when someone calls out, "It
hurts, man," Yuri turns back. Orfe can give him her faith in him,
but she cannot give him faith in himself.

Soon after, Orfe dies, like her namesake, while making her
music in a crowd. The mythical Orpheus is torn apart by women
who are driven to frenzy by his music. Orfe dies during a concert,
singing a new song with no words, a calling song. This is not one
of "Yuri's Dreams": "The crowd came closer, darker. . . . Orfe
called out from the top row of the bleachers . . . and all the dark
crowd seemed to wait for what would happen next, as she sang.
All the dark crowd seemed unable to wait, and it pressed in"
(115). The Graces become irrelevant and impotent, "losing their
hold on the music . . . swallowed up (115). Without any more

warning, the whole structure collapses, and Orfe falls to her death. Orfe has moved beyond the realm where the Graces can offer support; she falls into the black hole left by Yuri's inability to return to sobriety and to his life with her. After the funeral, Enny and the Graces go on with their lives, performing and sending Orfe's part of the royalties for "Yuri's Dreams" to Yuri's account. As far as Enny knows, Yuri never recovers.

While the plot of *Orfe* is closely aligned to the myth of Orpheus and Eurydice, Voigt uses the fairy tale "The Frog Prince" to elucidate the main theme of the novel. In the Grimms' version, a young princess is playing with her golden ball in the garden near a well. When the ball rolls into the well, the princess starts to weep. "What will you give me if I fetch up your ball?" asks a frog, "stretching his thick ugly head out of the water." The princess offers him even the golden crown that she wears, but the frog will have none of it. "If thou wouldst love me, and have me for thy companion and play-fellow . . . and sleep in thy little bed, . . . I would fetch thee thy golden ball again." The princess agrees, impatiently and impetuously, but, when her lovely ball, symbolizing a fully realized life, is retrieved, she ignores the frog and tries to leave him behind. The frog follows her home and actually climbs in her bed. She feels "beside herself with rage, and picking him up, she threw him with all her strength against the wall. . . . But as he fell, he ceased to be a frog, and became all at once a prince with beautiful kind eyes."[17] The two marry and are carried off to his father's kingdom, accompanied by the faithful Henry, the servant of the faithful prince, who has been obliged to wear three iron bands over his heart to contain his sorrow at his master's plight. The bands break, one by one, and now Henry is "relieved and happy," like his master and his new bride.

The young Orfe and Enny discuss the story. "'He was a frog, and that's slimy and cold,' Orfe said. 'I wouldn't want any frog sleeping on my pillow . . .'" (9). In his interpretation of fairy tales, Bruno Bettelheim thinks that the frog's transformation symbolizes the developmental process of the child "from a lower to a higher state of being,"[18] especially the child's sexual development.

Most young children, like Orfe and Enny, find the idea of both physical and emotional intimacy rather repulsive. This fear is a normal mode of self-protection against premature experiences.

"If I make a promise, I ought to keep it," says Enny, constrained by social principles and propriety. Acutely conscious of the possibilities of pain and cruelty, Enny is reluctant to grasp the messier parts of life, to engage in the joys and pains of living fully. Conjuring up the image of the princess hurling the helpless frog against the wall, she flinches at the thought of so much anger. Bettelheim interprets this part of the story as the decision to overcome fear and to enter fully and independently into relationships with others: "In a way this story tells that to be able to love, a person first has to be able to feel; even if the feelings are negative, that is better than not feeling. . . . At the end she asserts her independence in going against [her father's] orders. As she thus becomes herself, so does the frog; it turns into a prince" (Bettelheim, 288).

Orfe's goal is to live fully, to grapple with life and create truths of her own, to love: "But it's not about the frog, it's about the ball, the way the ball is perfect. If I had a golden ball and it was perfect, I'd promise anything to get it back. . . . He couldn't have turned into a prince if it wasn't for the golden ball Enny. The perfect thing" (*Orfe*, 10). In the first chapter, Orfe shows Enny how to assert herself against the boys who taunt her; Enny literally splits the skin of Rab by throwing her lunchbox at him, breaking herself free from her emotional repression and timidity. In the second chapter, it is Orfe who needs help. She is following the orders of the bandleader Jack, who, denying her talent, encourages her to vomit to fulfill the needs of the audience. Enny, dressed in her "interview suit," helps Orfe form her own band, facing down Jack as well as other professionals in the music band. Yuri "splits his skin" by undergoing rehab and rejecting an invitation to return to the drug house.

For a while, Yuri and Orfe seem to have "the perfect thing," a love that lets them both assert their talents independently, each supporting the other with love and faith. But when Yuri is poisoned with the drugged frosting on their wedding day, it falls apart. Orfe follows him to the drug house to try to save him, but it is another world: "It was like being underwater." Yuri turns back, failing to emerge from this "house of death" because "somebody tells him that it hurts. . . . What kind of fools are they if they think life is never going to hurt. If they think they can be safe and never hurt and still be alive?" asks Orfe. "Can you imagine it?" (120). Like the frog in Stevie Smith's poem, "The Frog Prince," Yuri is content to withdraw into the "enchantment" of drugs and vicarious experience, content to let others bear the pain of true love and life:

> I can be happy until you come
> But I cannot be heavenly,
> Only disenchanted people
> Can be heavenly.[19]

"The Frog Prince," in Bettelheim's interpretation, implies that maturity and the ability to become intimate with others happens once and forever. Voigt, however, believes that character development is an ongoing process, necessitating many acts of courage to break out of former definitions of self. In this novel, Voigt is portraying the power of a friend's faith—or love—to provide that courage. Just as Orfe gave Enny courage to make that first step, to express her anger at Rab and the others, Enny gives courage to Orfe to form her own band and, finally, despite her great fear and distress, to go to the house to save Yuri. Voigt dedicates this novel to her husband, Walter, "because it's a love story," a love story about Orfe and Yuri, but more, about Orfe and Enny, whose faith in each other enable each to live and love. "Can you imagine [a life without pain]?" asks Orfe. "Yes," says Enny. Like Yuri, she struggles, to live fully and independently, to keep faith in herself. But while he never does go on with his life, she does. In the split-second before she dies, Orfe sends a message to Enny: "Don't be afraid" (115). Enny understands: "Love stories aren't about how they end" (116).

Does this book work for readers who do not know the myth of Orpheus or the fairy tale about the frog prince? For some adolescent readers, the poetic texture of the language is enough. "I like it because it sounds like the way I talk and write and think. . . . I read it twice."[20] The story line is a collection of vignettes, arranged to mirror free association of thought rather than strict chronology. The narrator Enny is remembering the sequence of her thoughts about Orfe rather than the sequence of events. Each word or image leads into another subject: "We played endless games of cribbage . . . leapfrogging our markers around the tracks. He was a frog, and that's slimy and cold" (9). Yuri is introduced in the same way. Enny is describing how she became Orfe's manager, and suddenly Yuri's name pops up. "Orfe never lost patience, never lost hope, never lost faith in me. . . . I finally asked her about Yuri and she told me" (40). The five chapters each chronicle a step in the characters' relationships and refer forward or back to Yuri and Orfe's wedding day. While the first chapter establishes Orfe and Enny's friendship, the second lays out the whole plot, tracing the sequence of events from the time Orfe meets Yuri to the time after she dies and the "Graces are music history" (64). In the third chapter, Voigt describes the depth of Orfe and Yuri's love for each other. The fourth chapter is the story of their wedding day, when Yuri disappears, and of Orfe's subsequent death. In the fifth chapter, a mere three-page coda, Enny recalls a conversation in which Orfe recognizes the worth of Enny's supportive friendship and wonders that some people would prefer avoiding pain to living. It briefly restates the theme from "The Frog Prince" that has been played out in the plot of Orpheus and Eurydice. Although this book is about the pain of deeply felt love and the yearning to be released from that pain, it is also an affirmation of how loving friends give support and strength. Even those adolescents who do not recognize all the allusions to mythology and legend will recognize ties to their own experience in this universal story.

"In this bravura effort [Voigt] harnesses the strength of the myth to advance her own imaginative vision," writes Diane Roback in her highly favorable review (Roback, 125). *Orfe* is neither a retelling of the myth, nor of the fairy tale, but a powerful allegory using images from both to illustrate themes common in

Voigt's work: self-development does take courage and effort and is necessary for lasting and satisfying love—"Don't be afraid." Voigt invents a new story to renovate the powerful messages of the traditional legends. This is a novel that stretches both the imaginative and logical faculties of the mind, each pulling at the other to form a more complete understanding of a message that is more than logical. Myths are invented to preserve the mysteries of important truths, and, as Roback indicates in her review, in writing *Orfe*, Voigt may be more of a maker of new myths than a preserver of old ones.

When She Hollers (1994)

Like *Orfe*, *When She Hollers* uses a deceptively simple plot to explore the complexity of human relationships. At the beginning of the one day that the book describes, Tish, not quite eighteen, threatens her stepfather, Tonnie, with a knife she has recently bought. Tonnie has been abusing her sexually for a long time, and now she dares to ask him to stop. She feels that if she can get the truth out, she will be free from him, but her mother, busy with breakfast for her three younger children, will not hear. Frustrated but not quite defeated, Tish refuses to go to her room as Tonnie orders and starts to walk to school.

Her courage—or perhaps it is desperation—comes from the recent suicide of Miranda, a fat, homely, pregnant schoolmate who was found hanging naked from a tree in front of her home. Randy, as her schoolmates called her, supposedly had approached a number of boys asking for sex, but Tish suspects that Miranda has been the victim of her father, who drove her to school and picked her up each day; Tish had watched Miranda "lumbering out the doors and down the sidewalk to where the car waited . . . like a girl going down the hallway to the electric chair every day."[21] Tish had guessed that Miranda had it worse, and, secretly relieved, she had been silent instead of trying to connect with the unattractive girl. Perhaps Miranda had hanged herself publicly to punish her father, but when Tish hints this to her mother or her friends, no one even wants to face the possibility of incest. In the end, Miranda has not been vindicated.

On the way to school, Tish dons a tough and fearless demeanor, separating herself from the scared, defenseless victim of the previous night. Today she has her "survival knife" tucked into her right boot. Perhaps *this* can keep her safe—unless what Tonnie has said is right—that she would be jailed for felonious assault if she defended herself. Her English teacher, Mrs. Wyse (an obvious pun), has written on the board, "The truth shall set you free," and today Tish has decided to voice that truth. But fear makes this task difficult. She must push "the reluctant words up out of her throat to stand in a row . . . facing him" (1). Although Tonnie is furiously angry, he can control himself, confusing her with his "Daddy voice" (4), making her wonder for a moment if she is crazy, imagining the awful things he does. Later in the day, when her gym teacher tries to pull the shoe off that is hiding her survival knife, it is Tish's voice that both betrays her and reveals her truth. Losing control, she lets out the scream that she has been controlling forever, the scream that Tonnie has kept in her by covering her mouth, the scream that is always muffled by the sounds of the TV so that her mother will not have to hear. When the coach pages Mrs. Wyse, Tish feels a moment of safety, but her favorite teacher, sympathetic in so many ways, is afraid to hear the words Tish forces out: "Wait. . . . You can really do damage with some the things you can say, Tish. . . . You have to think about the consequences" (76); she refuses to let Tish continue. Tish's voice fades away with her courage, "getting smaller and smaller, and if she opened her mouth to say something, she would weep and cry" (77).

The next stop is to see the principal, a well-meaning man whose voice changes pitch, betraying his nervousness. Tish feels safe and in control again until he tells her that he has called in her stepfather. Terrified, Tish runs away, her mind splintering from sensible thought. In her terror she barely hears the voice of her friend Chrissie, who tells her to visit her lawyer father, Mr. Battle. Afraid that she will end up like Miranda, Tish struggles against the fear and distrust that threaten to stifle her. She is finally able to tell the truth after Mr. Battle names his own troubles, speaking to her as a peer. By asking Tish for a fee, Mr. Battle becomes her lawyer and is able to protect her voice and give her the power of law over Tonnie.

Naming is a key that recurs in many forms in the story. Tonnie has humiliated Tish by rearranging the letters of her name to spell and mean "shit." Tish insists that her friends use Miranda's whole name rather than the double-entendre "Randy." Now, as Tish sits in Mr. Battle's office deciding to tell him the truth, she thinks of the fairy tale Rumpelstiltskin, where only the power of naming the gnome-like figure can save the girl-queen's child. Tish remembers that in that story the father had also lied about his daughter and made her helpless until she was saved by the benevolent hunter who could discover the right name for her enemy. In *The Uses of Enchantment*, Bettelheim writes that the hunter denotes "the subjugation of the animal, asocial, violent tendencies in man—an eminently protective figure who can and does save us from the dangers of our own violent emotions and those of others" (Bettelheim, 206). Now the lawyer Battle acts as the hunter for Tish, naming Tonnie's actions "rape" and planning out a strategy to protect her from Miranda's fate.

Mr. Battle is the first adult in Tish's life who honors her voice, listening to her version of the truth and preserving her words in writing as a weapon against Tonnie's threats. His acceptance of her version as sane and true allows her to believe that there is more to her life than the body that Tonnie abuses. He has given her access to the power of language to define her life. In a sense, the truth has set Tish free, yet, ironically, she has had to lie about her age, saying that she is eighteen, to let Mr. Battle advise and protect her as an adult. Voigt's message is that the current formulation of the law prevents children from freely telling the truth to adults who could help them.

As Tish returns to her house, where Tonnie is waiting, she is armed with her knife, her lawyer, and her vision of herself as whole, but she senses the storm waiting for her, "the door bulging out with all the fury behind it" (121). All Tish has is "reason to hope . . . , but this is better news than Tish had heard for all of her life" (119). This novel can be read as an inversion of Shakespeare's *The Tempest*. Whereas Prospero uses his magic to complete his daughter's education and to find a princely companion for her, Tonnie, like the magician who creates the illusion of sawing the girl in half, uses his paternal power to separate the truth of his horrible actions at night from his role of kind father by day. While Prospero celebrates his daughter's beauty, protects her chastity, and shows her a new world of beauty in humans, Tonnie shames Tish, listing the ugliness he sees in her, sullying her body, and questioning her sanity. In the end, while Shakespeare's Miranda accompanies her new lover to a new world where her father will be king, Tish must return alone to the stormy house of her father, who has no power elsewhere. The Miranda of Tish's story has not been able to survive the stormy island of her father's home, but she has inspired Tish to save her own life. Of course, Voigt's most important inversion of *The Tempest* is her vision of the daughter as the heroic central character—who must learn to "holler" and to take action for herself.

In *When She Hollers*, Voigt has written a powerful handbook for young people who suffer from abuse. Tish survives by separating her inner self from the physical victim, by insisting that her voice be heard, and finally, by courageously reaching out to an adult with the power to help protect her. What Tish wants is safety and self-respect. Her courage gives her hope.

7. Voigt's Essential Ideas: A Thematic Overview

For Cynthia Voigt, the main advantage of writing books is that she can start a unique conversation with her readers: "One bases one's life on certain essential ideas about [its] nature and purpose . . . , but seldom do these essential ideas, which in fact govern choices and actions, receive direct attention" (Voigt, *Horn Book*, 401). In her novels, Voigt pays deep and direct attention to many ideas through the mouths and minds of her characters, who reflect on the implications of what they read, hear, and experience. Insofar as her protagonists mirror her own values, it is evident that this author prizes thoughtfulness and curiosity as vital to personal development and that Cynthia Voigt the teacher is still reaching out to her readers/students, urging them to think about these ideas that govern choices and action.

Voigt believes that men and women should be able to develop their potential unconstrained by conventional assumptions about who they should be. Her novels deal with the struggles of young women and men to achieve individuality in the context of the social world in which they live, and they portray this ageless quest in language that is informative and thought-provoking. Her protagonists overcome their fear of the unknown, realizing their separateness as individual identities, independent from and yet also responsive to their family or historical situations. Either by accident or by choice, Voigt's heroes "reach out" from the closed circle of familiar assumptions and values to the realm of other possibilities. As they explore these challenging options, learning what is possible, they also learn to "hold on" to what is valuable, especially family roots.

Finally Voigt's characters struggle with "letting go," balancing the extent of self-fulfillment with responsibility to others as they respond to the possibilities that fate provides. At the end of *Seventeen Against the Dealer*, the last of the Tillerman series, Dicey sums up what individuals need in order to fulfill their potential: "Then she understood—it wasn't guarantees she needed, or any of them needed, but chances, chances to take. Just the chance to take a chance. And the eye to recognize it, she added. The hand, to reach out and hold onto it—that too. And the heart, or the stomach, or wherever courage came from" (209). These are some of Voigt's essential ideas.

Stepping Beyond Conventional Roles

The search for self-identity is a traditional theme in literature, but until the last century, most protagonists who left home to make an independent quest were white, middle-class males. Traditionally, female characters defined their identities as lovers, wives, mothers, or sisters who served and waited for the male adventurer. Their roles were dependent on the fate of the male hero, and they were more passive than men, who actively shaped their own destiny. Characters from lower-class backgrounds were often "rescued" by marriage to a handsome prince or by suddenly discovering a connection to wealth or aristocracy. Voigt's novels follow a trend in literature for young adults beginning with works like Louisa May Alcott's *Little Women* (1868), in which female protagonists make choices that recognize the possibility of an active and autonomous identity (Murphy, 1990), depending more on their skill and abilities to work than on romance.

In 1970, a study titled *Sexism in Children's Books* examined a thousand general trade books that had received either an award or official recognition for excellence. The study found that only one-fifth presented a positive image of women. Most depicted situations in which girls had to choose between femininity and strength, or between love and a professional career, as if no compromise could be reached. The two hundred exceptions were deemed acceptable as nonsexist because they "illustrate the blossoming of a female individual without any concern for conformity."[1]

Nonsexist literature, however, does not just portray girls who are nonconformist. It is literature that reflects the complex totality of individual humans rather than fostering the stereotypical assumptions people make when they generalize from superficial observation. The editors of *A Guide to Non-sexist Children's Books*, published in 1987, write: "The subject matter of the last decade has given way to the more complex observations of struggle, growth, and change that are the constants of real life. The books included in the *Guide* might be best characterized as role-free; many *are* about strong women and forthright young girls, but others are about thoughtful boys or troubled young people of either sex who, through experience and thoughtful observation, learn how to solve their problems independently."[2] Of the six hundred titles cited as nonsexist from all the books for children and young adults published between 1976 and 1985, three of Voigt's novels were chosen: *Homecoming, Dicey's Song*, and *A Solitary Blue*.

Voigt has identified herself as more humanist than feminist: "I believe there are real differences between the sexes, but we are all human beings and so have a lot in common; it seems to me that shared *humanity* is crucial in storytelling" (Commire, 224). Yet she feels that "women and girls need to be careful about believing what they are told about themselves" (Bennett, 13). Much of what is shared in her books centers on the struggles of her characters to form individual identities in a world where conventional roles prove inadequate to cope with unusual circumstances. Both the female and the male heroes of her books act from the identities they are inventing for themselves rather than react from conventional perspectives. This tendency is central to most feminist philosophies, which demand at least a choice of behavior among the possible social roles, a "blossoming of a female individual without any concern for conformity" (Castro, 238). Voigt's definition of humanism incorporates the precepts of feminism and applies them with a broader brush: her characters are nonsexist because they act and react as complex individuals rather than as gender-based stereotypes.

The Feminist Press, founded in 1970 to produce and foster literature for older children and young adults, proposed five criteria for nonsexist literature that provide a useful framework to discuss the characteristic inclusiveness of Voigt's novels, a tendency to allow her protagonists a wide range of possibilities.

Girls are active protagonists.

Voigt's heroines are not only active but leaders, demonstrating great courage, intelligence, and physical stamina to overcome a variety of obstacles. In *Tell Me If the Lovers Are Losers*, which includes no major male characters, Ann, Niki, and Hildy become stronger individuals and bond into a working team like the protagonists of traditionally male sports novels, without the romance and gossipy competition of many "female" novels. The same kind of cooperative teamwork is evident in *Orfe* when Orfe, the three Graces (one of them male), and Enny form a rock group. In various novels of the Tillerman series, Dicey is clearly the leader of her family, making the necessary decisions to lead them to a safe home. The heroines of Voigt's two mysteries, *The Callender Papers* and *The Vandemark Mummy*, both find solutions by studying texts that have mystified adults. Gwyn, of *Jackaroo*, performs all the deeds of a typical swashbuckler hero, with all of the swagger, too. Birle in *On Fortune's Wheel* rescues *her* prince from imprisonment and nurses him back to health. Even Izzy of *Izzy, Willy-Nilly* and Alexis of *Glass Mountain*, who begin as obedient daughters, learn to make their own decisions.

Boys express a wide range of emotions.

Perhaps the only flat, single-sided male in Voigt's novels is Rudyard, the unrelievedly evil tomato farmer who threatens the children in *Homecoming*. In *The Runner*, the angry Bullet has many characteristics of the conventional "tough guy," protecting himself from further rejection with scornful silence, physical self-discipline, and outbursts of violence; yet Voigt also shows the tender hopes he has for his mother. Readers of the Tillerman series see James and Sammy pass through a number of emotional steps as they mature. Fearful and self-conscious as a boy, James develops into an intellectually courageous young man. Sammy is, by turns, exuberant, stubborn, impatient, and thoughtful; a sturdy worker and athlete, he is perhaps the person that his Uncle Bullet could have been, had he been nurtured by a loving family. Voigt's male characters also include the fastidious and glamorous Gregor in *Glass Mountain*; the intellectually brilliant Jonathan and his more cautious friend Henry of *David and Jonathan*; the faithful hired man, Burl, of *Jackaroo*, who is more sensitive than Gwyn at first realizes; and Orien, the prince of *On Fortune's Wheel*, who gives up his rights to royal leisure in order to live simply and independently. In her depiction of each of these males, Voigt portrays a range of emotions and motivations so that each becomes memorable as an individual personality.

Boys and girls engage in noncompetitive friendships.

Away from her familiar home and afraid for her physical safety, Jean Callender is comforted by her friendship with Oliver McWilliams, a friendship based on mutual respect without an ounce of romance. Oliver tells Jean the history of her family, and she, in turn, tutors him in Latin. This exchange of strengths is typical of the mutually supportive relationships Voigt portrays between male and female friends and siblings. Dicey depends on James to help her think out solutions, and, in turn, James helps Maybeth figure out how to improve her reading. Dicey's friendship with Jeff grows into the best kind of romantic partnership, in which each encourages the other to develop individual strengths. In contrast, Gregor of *Glass Mountain*, playing the traditional role of the predatory male in his pursuit of the mysterious Alexis, fails to catch her; their relationship works only after he stops pursuing her and they become friends.

Children relate to adults.

In many novels for young adults, female heroes find guidance and support from adults in their lives, but in Voigt's stories, adults often prove inadequate and unresponsive to their children's needs. In *A Solitary Blue, The Runner*, and *Sons from Afar*, books in the Tillerman series, Voigt portrays male characters who unsuccessfully seek help and support from their parents as they develop their own identities. More often, though, Voigt's children relate to adult characters in helpful partnerships. After she has given Dicey a much-needed respite, Gram insists that she share again the responsibilities for figuring out what is best for their family. Bullet learns wisdom from his employer and mentor, Patrice, just as Althea of *The Vandemark Mummy* learns about classical culture from her father, who shares his knowledge and assumes that she can understand. Brann of *Building Blocks* and Clothilde of *Tree by Leaf* virtually direct their families toward brighter futures. Through these relationships, Voigt indicates her great respect for the capacities of children to understand and contribute to the adult world.

The literature deals with various patterns of living and themes such as single parenthood, divorce, extended family, multiracial families, adoption, handicaps, death, and nontraditional careers.

Like most other writers of young adult literature since the 1960s, Voigt recognizes that childhood as a time of innocence and safety is a fiction available only to a privileged few. Her novels deal with the hard facts of single parenthood (*The Vandemark Mummy* and *A Solitary Blue*), divorce (*A Solitary Blue*), extended family (*Homecoming*), racial prejudice (*Come a Stranger, The Runner*), adoption (*Homecoming*), handicaps (*Izzy, Willy-Nilly, Tree by Leaf*), incest (*When She Hollers*), death (*Dicey's Song, David and Jonathan*) and nontraditional careers (*Seventeen Against the Dealer*). She faces these hard facts straight on, probing in detail the difficult implications that can arise out of these circumstances.

As single parents, the professor fathers in *The Vandemark Mummy* and *A Solitary Blue* both suffer excruciating guilt when their children are endangered; Cousin Eunice and then Gram struggle with financial and emotional burdens when four young children suddenly intrude upon their lives. As an African-American, Mina faces the rejection of her fellow dancers at the ballet camp; and, as a white, Bullet wrestles with his own habits of prejudicial thinking. Izzy learns to live without a leg and Clothilde, without her father's smile. The Tillermans accept their mother's death, and Henry and Jonathan grope toward an understanding of David's suicide. Each of these characters faces serious obstacles and responds with varying degrees of understanding and capacity for growth. Yet Voigt implies that, regardless of the limitations of fate, all people have strengths and should be given the opportunity to respond to the accidents of their lives with choices that develop these strengths. What is necessary is not just the chance to reach beyond conventional options but also the opportunity to learn the comparative value of these possibilities.

The Eye to Discern: The Importance of Questioning

Traditionally, fictional literature has emphasized the physical appearance of its protagonists as symbolic of their moral values: readers who were familiar with the conventional signals of their culture could predict the moral tenor of main characters, particularly of female protagonists, from the author's physical descriptions. Either the heroine is idealized as perfect in both body and spirit, or she is stereotypically cast into the pretty/plain dichotomy where heroines who do not embody current standards of beauty are portrayed as "undervalued, unglamorous, but animated"[3] and are unusually virtuous. Voigt's characterizations of her protagonists stem mostly from what goes on in their minds, either as revealed through dialogue or in direct exposition; it is evident that she values the inner qualities of people more than their outward appearances. When she does describe physical appearances, she is more apt to focus on the physical attractions of her male protagonists. While readers know that Dicey never gets tired of looking at Jeff, "beautiful, inside and out," and that

Burl has a "dark beard, dark eyes, and olive complexion," there is little celebration of the female characters' physical beauty.

We know only that Dicey is tough and wiry, dressing in boys' clothes to build boats and that Gwyn is strong and sturdy. What is most important to Voigt is the character of the person underneath the superficial appearance. Although Alexis is initially attracted to Gregor because he appears to be the kind of wealthy upper-class gentleman she needs to satisfy her parents, it is, ironically, only after she learns to appreciate the basic character revealed in his guise as butler that she comes to love him and dares to make a lasting commitment—and then discovers that he is, indeed, more suitable to her station in life than she ever expected.

Like many adolescents, Voigt's characters find that their first attractions are superficial and end in disappointment. Jean is attracted to the playful Mr. Callender; Jeff to lovely Melody; Mina, to the world of ballet; Gywn, to the role of the Jackaroo; and Birle, to a life of royal ease. But Jean and Jeff and Mina find that facile grace and brilliant surfaces can hide a cruel self-centeredness that excludes real emotional commitment. Gwyn's costume constrains her from finding her real strengths, and Birle finds that a life without work is boring.

Some of Voigt's characters look for parents, especially those who are absent, to help in their search for an identity. But absent parents prove inadequate; they provide no magic answer. Children cannot adopt the identities of their parents as their own. Nothing can substitute for each individual's struggle to learn about his or her social context and to develop skills necessary to grow into an autonomous adult able to make choices.

Voigt believes that this growth is fueled by thoughtful intelligence, the willingness to dig beyond the easy answers and to comprehend the complexity of people and their environments. Success comes not from luck or fate, but from stretching the imagination toward new possibilities and learning new skills. Several of her characters are scholars, using academic skills to ferret out answers to their questions: Ann Gardner studies the classical canon of Western tradition; Jean Thiel pores over family documents; Dicey's brother James thinks about the things he hears and reads; and Jonathan can quote the Talmud with ease. Gwyn and Birle defy the law of their medieval world to learn to read, and that knowledge saves their lives. The academic side of Voigt is evident not only in her favorable portrayal of characters with curious minds but also in her many literary allusions, ranging from Shakespeare's plays and *The Odyssey* to fairy tales like "Hansel and Gretel," "Rumpelstiltskin," and "The Frog Prince."

While her respect for the kind of traditional knowledge found in books and schools is evident, she also pays homage to the more intuitive analysis of experience and people, which is characteristic of Maybeth, Gram, Brann, Burl, and Clothilde. Hildy teaches Ann to look for the best in people; Maybeth is wise though she expresses her insights in simple language; and Clothilde learns from listening and watching the people and landscape of rural Maine. For Voigt, it is essential for a person to develop whatever mental skills are available to solve the problems at hand, actively studying experience as well as texts to construct new ideas for defining solutions. Learning and thinking are the way her characters perceive what to let go and what to hold onto.

The Hand to Reach Out: The Importance of Commitment

Identity achievement occurs after "significant occupational and ideological questioning" and subsequent commitment to work and other people, claims a recent psychologist of adolescent development.[4] Voigt's heroes succeed when they are open to learning the ideas and practicing the skills that will shape their futures *and* when they demonstrate the tenacity to make and keep commitments. In modern Western society, individuals are defined by what they do (work) and how they relate to others (love). The concept of work as a main source of individual fulfillment and self-actualization is historically recent,[5] and it is a concept that Voigt illustrates repeatedly in the development of her protagonists. They reflect the virtues of self-reliance and social

responsibility, virtues of the pre–Industrial Age when children
were "economically functional,"[6] just as they are becoming again
in the late twentieth century.

Voigt's protagonists are hard workers. Dicey and her brothers
and sister finally win their grandmother's grudging acceptance
into her home by working hard around her farm, proving their
diligence and usefulness. James and Sammy help with finances
by crabbing one summer, until James gets a job in a doctor's
office, one more suited to his nonathletic nature. Maybeth spends
many long hours struggling with her schoolwork as well as practicing the piano and cooking. Gwyn and Clothilde perform endless chores for their families, and Henry works for Jonathan's
father in their restaurant.

The characters in Voigt's novels who avoid commitment to
work prove disloyal in personal relationships, incapable of maturity as partners or as parents. Enoch Callender, dressed in his
white suits, spends his days imagining the future away; his wife's
money already spent, he expects to be supported by an inheritance that is not legally his. His greed for free money and his
avoidance of work are the root of the fear he engenders. Melody
claims to leave her son and husband in order to help alleviate the
poverty of the world; yet her "work" is haphazard and ineffective
because she flits from cause to cause and fails to face the world
and herself honestly. Francis Verricker, the faraway father of the
Tillerman children, is characterized as a master of avoiding work
and failing to pay debts. All these characters are brilliantly
charming and immediately attractive, but eventually they prove
untrustworthy. In *Orfe*, Yuri and his drummer friend are talented musicians, but, lacking the will to practice, to work through
the pain and effort of daily life, they sink into the deathlike world
of drugs. Voigt's theme in all of these books is that commitment
is necessary for growth, whether it be to the work of learning or
to the work of loving friends and family.

In Voigt's novels, the characters who choose their work enjoy
it. Dicey finds peace in sanding the sailboat in the barn after she
has led her family to Crisfield. After his muscles harden, Jeff
finds the hard work of crabbing therapeutic. Even when Birle is

▪ure out what is important to them and how they can achieve
▪ance of commitments between relationships and work. It is
▪ecessary nor even virtuous for her heroes to sacrifice them-
▪s to others. By thinking hard to imagine alternate possibili-
▪and making choices without the constraints of convention,
▪ achieve self-sufficiency without entrapping themselves or
▪rs. Voigt recognizes that it often takes great courage for
▪eloping individuals to overcome their initial fear of moving
▪ond the limiting assumptions of conventional society and to
▪ke binding commitments, but this courage is necessary for sat-
▪actory self-fulfillment.

The Heart or the Stomach to Be:
The Necessity for Courage

The dragon to be slain is the monster of the status quo: Hold-
▪ast, the keeper of the past," says Joseph Campbell in his book
▪bout literary and mythic heroes, *The Hero with a Thousand
Faces*.[7] For Voigt the real dragon is the fear of change, the fear of
▪meeting new experiences head on and learning from them. In
Tell Me If the Lovers Are Losers, Ann prefers being by herself to
any contact with strangers where she must struggle to "fit in";
only after she dares to ally herself with individuals who are
socially different, exploring values that distinguish her from her
upper-middle-class family, does she become comfortable with herself as a valid human being, capable of reaching out to new ideas
and experiences.

For Voigt, the conventional "nice" girl seems inauthentic, an
immature and unexplored self, unwilling to take the risks necessary to learn. She addresses this issue again in *Izzy, Willy-Nilly*
when Isobel ironically becomes a more whole person after losing
her leg, making her "different" but capable of authentic relationships with the very people she had previously admired only from
afar. She gathers the courage from her newfound friends to
admit her fears and her anger, confronting her friends and herself with truths that disturb their smooth social surface. Simi-

separated from her beloved Orien and miser
finds benefit in the never-ending toil. At first
tracting her mind and of forgetting, but late:
more adept, she appreciates the "pleasure o.
hands had done, and done well" (*On Fortune's
Voigt does not romanticize work. The Tillerma
unbearably hot and itchy as they pull down tl
vines from their grandmother's house. Jean Thi
and spirit hurt as she sorts what seem like endless
ly letters and papers. Dicey, Clothilde, Gwyn,
express a rebellious resentment against the constr
daily responsibilities and chores.

Sometimes it is not the commitment to work but
ships that detract from work that are irksome. In *h*
Dicey is annoyed when Sammy wants to talk while she
sailboat, and later, in *Seventeen Against the Dealer*,
trying to start her own boat-building business, she for
equal attention to Jeff and the rest of her family until s.
that she risks losing them. Jeff's father, the professor,
work shield him from the desperate need of his son for
ance and human care. Birle is almost sorry to see her l
Orien, appear after she has established herself on her far
she plans to grow herbs and prepare medicines, but then s
izes that they can both perform their independent work tog

Voigt explores the complications of making and keepin
mitments to both family and career in *Building Blocks*,
Brann's mother and father finally compromise so that bot
pursue their chosen work and remain together as a famil
The Vandemark Mummy, Phineas and Althea live with t
father near Portland, Maine, while their mother pursues a lu
tive position on the other side of the country in Portland, Oreg
While this decision seems to work temporarily, it causes hardsh
and loneliness for all members of the family; at the end of tl
book, Voigt makes no clear pronouncement on the long-ter
future of the family members' relationships to each other.

However, Voigt's protagonists are not martyrs suffering with
sweet passivity; they are whole personalities who use their brains

larly, in *Glass Mountain* (1991) Alexis fears disappointing her parents' expectation that she perpetuate their upper-middle-class traditions by marrying a suitable man. Only after Alexis dares flout the conventions of her parents' social world can she make a commitment based on the truth of her own needs and feelings.

In these instances, Ann, Isobel, and Alexis choose to emerge from the muffling protection of their families to explore different values and options. For other protagonists, circumstances allow little room to choose. Dicey's courage, after her mother abandons her and her siblings, is more a determination to find a new home for her family than a choice she could make. Clothilde too is at first driven by her sister and mother's need for sustenance. Gwyn's courageous decision to don the mask of Jackaroo is fueled by her horror at the injustices of her society and her desire to right the wrongs she sees. Because these characters perceive a need for someone to lead, they undertake adventures that demand the kind of courage that is the dogged persistence to continue, the decision to carry through a commitment for the sake of others. This courage, motivated by a strong sense of caring for others, is an important component of Voigt's vision of the way the world should be.

In *Building Blocks*, Brann learns that his father has this kind of courage, once he is given the first bit of encouragement. Like Dicey, who, after finding a home, must wait until she tries college to start her own adventure, Brann finds that courage can mean patience as well as persistence. Phineas must call upon reserves of this kind when he is searching the library basement for his missing sister, Althea. It is brave persistence that helps Henry remain loyal to Jonathan despite David's efforts to separate them. This type of courage is not particularly splashy nor evident to others, yet it is a sign and a source of tremendous strength, especially when practiced over a long period of time.

Voigt illustrates the insidious danger of fear most explicitly in *Orfe* and *When She Hollers*. When Yuri, Orfe's lover and new husband, retreats into the drug world where he and his friends can avoid facing the painful realities of the real world, they also lose the love and glory of real relationships. As a child, Enny had shrunk in teary fright from the litany of terrors that her school-mates had used to taunt her; her new friendship with Orfe gives her the courage to express her rage and assert herself as more than just another victim. With this fear gone, she can join Orfe in her career to sing so anyone can understand and join in: "Don't be afraid," signals Orfe as she dies. In *When She Hollers*, Tish senses herself on the edge of suicidal despair, but she drags her-self out of silence, where no one knows the truth about her step-father's abuse of her, buys a knife, and finally shares her story with a lawyer. For Voigt, overcoming the fear of exploring new options is essential to becoming and staying alive.

Putting It All Together

For Voigt, these essential elements of self-realization are not sep-arate chronological steps but interrelated parts of a recursive cycle. Courage to reach out is, in part, derived from holding on to a nurturing relationship with family and friends. Letting go is the ability to take a chance, fueled by new skills and insights to move toward new possibilities yet ballasted by old strengths and roots. Though Dicey gradually lets go of her responsibilities for raising her siblings, she remains a part of the family, recognizing the ability of Maybeth and Sammy to let her know when she is needed to help them care for Gram. Jonathan lets go of his guilt over David's suicide yet retains his memory of the suffering that he represents. This memory gives him the strength necessary to endure his own suffering as a war prisoner in Vietnam. Both know that they will have a chance to reach out again to new opportunities, made stronger and wiser by each new experience, knowing more clearly what to hold on to, whom to reach out for, when to let go again. The cycle should never end: Voigt has declared "learning, not knowing, is what it's about" (Donelson and Nilsen, 376).

In Voigt's work, the nexus of characters and events is how the reader learns her essential ideas. Her view of life is a broadly humanist one, respecting the possibilities in all humans who have the courage to explore, the humility to listen to other ideas, the wisdom to value responsibilities to family and friends, and the energy to work for a personal dream. None of Voigt's heroes is a martyr. Unlike traditional morality which, especially for women, teaches selflessness, Voigt's ideal is self-definition, an independence based on the acknowledged support of loving relationships that do not seek to limit or dominate the other. "You have to let people be who they are," says Sammy in *Sons from Afar* (80), and "You can only be what you are" (95). These simple but hard-won insights—achieved with the help of courage, education, experience, and support—are some of Cynthia Voigt's essential ideas.

Notes and References

1. Cynthia Voigt: Adventurer Beneath the Surface

1. Anne Commire, ed., *Something about the Author* (Detroit: Gale, 1987), 220; hereafter cited in the text.

2. Don Gallo, *Speaking for Ourselves* (Urbana, Ill.: National Council of Teachers of English, 1990), 217; hereafter cited in the text.

3. L. Metzger and D. Straub, eds., *Contemporary Authors: New Revision Series* (Detroit: Gale, 1986), 468; hereafter cited in the text.

4. Cynthia Voigt, "Newbery Acceptance Speech," *Horn Book*, August 1983, 8; hereafter cited in the text.

5. Dorothy Kauffman, "Profile: Cynthia Voigt." *Language Arts*, December 1985, 877; hereafter cited in the text.

6. Virginia Monseau and Gary Salvner, *Reading Their World* (Portsmouth, N.H.: Heinemann, 1992), 33.

7. Kenneth Donelson and Aileen Pace Nilsen, *Literature for Today's Young Adults* (Glenview, Ill.: Scott, Foresman, 1989), 376; hereafter cited in the text.

8. Carol Pearson and Katherine Pope, *The Female Hero* (New York: R. R. Bowker, 1981), viii.

9. Kay Vandergrift, unpublished interview with Cynthia Voigt, September 1989.

2. Looking Beneath the Tip of the Iceberg: Defining the Self

1. Cynthia Voigt, *Callender Papers* (New York: Atheneum, 1983), 1.

2. Gerald Senick and Melissa Hug, *Children's Literature Review* (Detroit: Gale Research, 1987), 224.

3. Michelle Slung, "Adolescent Heroes," *Book World*, 8 May 1983, 14.

4. Ethel Heins, *Horn Book*, August 1983, 458.

5. Robin McKinley, *Children's Book Review Service*, Spring 1983, 128.

6. *Kirkus Reviews*, 15 March 1983, 308.

7. William Shakespeare, *The Merchant of Venice*, III.7.65.

8. Claire Rosser, *Kliatt Young Adult Paperbook Guide*, 17 September 1983, 20.

9. Cynthia Voigt, *Tell Me If the Lovers Are Losers*, (New York: Atheneum, 1982), 1.

10. Sally Estes, *Booklist*, 15 March 1982, 950; Rosser, 20.

11. Joe McKenzie, *School Library Journal*, 28 May 1982, 88.

12. Kathleen Leverich, *New York Times Book Review*, 10 May 1982, 38; hereafter cited in the text.

3. Reaching Out, Holding On, and Letting Go: Self-Development in Cynthia Voigt's Tillerman Series

1. This chapter, in briefer form, first appeared as "Images in Cynthia Voigt's Tillerman Series," *ALAN Review*, Fall 1991, 10–14.

2. Cynthia Voigt, *Homecoming* (New York: Atheneum, 1981), 7.

3. Cynthia Voigt, *Dicey's Song* (New York: Atheneum, 1982), 5.

4. Cynthia Voigt, *A Solitary Blue* (New York: Atheneum, 1983), 45.

5. Debra Robertson, *Portraying Persons with Disabilities: An Annotated Bibliography of Fiction for Children and Teenagers* (Providence, N.J.: R. R. Bowker, 1992), 397.

6. Christine Behrman, *School Library Journal*, 2 October 1986, 184.

7. K. Beetz and S. Niemeyer, eds., *Beacham's Guide to Literature For Young Adults* (New York: Beacham, 1989), 338–39.

8. Beth Nelms, Ben Nelms, and Linda Horton, "Broken Circles: Adolescents on Their Own," *English Journal*, September 1985, 84; Roger Sutton, *Bulletin of the Center for Children's Books*, October 1986, 40, hereafter cited in the text; Kathleen Goodin, *Interracial Books for Children Bulletin*, 1985, 16.

9. David Bennett, "Authorgraph No. 66: Cynthia Voigt," *Books for Keeps*, 1 January 1991, 13; hereafter cited in the text.

10. Gloria Rohmann, *School Library Journal*, September 1983, 140.

11. Jane Langton, *New York Times Book Review*, 27 November 1983, 34; hereafter cited as Langton.

12. Judith Plotz, "The Disappearance of Childhood: Parent-Child Role Reversals in *After the First Death* and *A Solitary Blue*," *Children's Literature in Education*, 1988, 12.

13. Gloria Jameson, "The Triumphs of the Spirit in Cynthia Voigt's *Homecoming, Dicey's Song*, and *A Solitary Blue*," in *Triumphs of the Spirit in Children's Literature*, ed. Francelia Butler and Richard Rotert (New York: Library Professional Publications, 1986), 3.

14. James Henke, "Dicey, Odysseus, and Hansel and Gretel: The Lost Children in Voigt's *Homecoming*," *Children's Literature in Education*, Spring 1985, 50.

15. Zena Sutherland, *Bulletin of the Center for Children's Books*, October 1982, 38; Denise Wilms, *Booklist*, September 1982, 50.

16. Ronald Jobe, *Language Arts*, November 1983, 1025; Langton, 34.

17. Elizabeth Colwell, *The Junior Bookshelf*, June 1984, 147; Marilyn Kaye, *School Library Journal*, April 1981, 144; Ruth Stein, *Language Arts*, January 1982, 55.

18. Karen Klockner, *Horn Book*, August 1981, 439.

19. Ethel Twichell, *Horn Book*, November 1986, 749.

4. Learning to Live: Ways of Knowing

1. Part of this chapter appeared in *Signal*, Fall 1992, 6–10.

2. M. Belenky, B. Clinchy, N. Goldberger, and J. Tarule, *Women's Ways of Knowing: The Development of Self, Voice, and Mind* (New York: Basic Books, 1986), 15; hereafter cited in the text.

3. Cynthia Voigt, *Izzy, Willy-Nilly* (New York: Atheneum, 1986), 209.

4. Pat Thomson, *Books for Keeps*, July 1992, 26.

5. Patty Campbell, *Wilson Library Bulletin*, November 1986, 49.

6. *Bulletin of the Center for Children's Books*, May 1986, 179; Mary Lou Burket, *Book World*, 11 May 1986, 17.

7. *Books for Keeps*, July 1989, 12; *Publisher's Weekly*, 25 April 1986, 79.

8. Cynthia Voigt, *Building Blocks* (New York: Atheneum, 1984), 30.

9. Zena Sutherland, *Bulletin of the Center for Children's Books*, April 1984, 158.

10. Mary Burns, *Horn Book*, August 1984, 470.

11. Frances Bradburn, *Wilson Library Bulletin*, June 1988, 109.

12. Elizabeth Watson, *Horn Book*, May 1988, 363.

13. Terry Ley, *English Journal*, March 1990, 80.

14. Cynthia Voigt, *The Vandemark Mummy* (New York: Atheneum, 1991), 184.

15. Jim Brewbaker, *ALAN Review*, Fall 1992, 23; *Publisher's Weekly*, 9 August 91, 58.

16. Zena Sutherland, *Bulletin of the Center for Children's Books*, September 91, 24; Elizabeth Watson, *Horn Book*, November 1991, 741.

5. Heroic Ventures

1. Mary Burns, *Horn Book*, March 1986, 210.

2. Patty Campbell, *Wilson Library Bulletin*, March 1986, 50.

3. Cynthia Voigt, *Jackaroo* (Atheneum, 1985), 54.

4. *Publisher's Weekly*, 9 August 1985, 77.

5. *Bulletin of the Center for Children's Books*, September 1985, 19.

6. Barbara Samuels, *ALAN Review*, Winter 1991, 24.

7. Cynthia Voigt, *On Fortune's Wheel* (New York: Atheneum, 1990), 22.

8. Ann Flowers, *Horn Book*, May 1990, 341; Susan Hepler, *School Library Journal*, March 1990, 242.

9. Victor Watson, *Times Educational Supplement*, 17 May 1991, 28.

10. Roger Sutton, *Bulletin of the Center for Children's Books*, July 1990, 276.

11. Cynthia Voigt, *The Wings of A Falcon* (New York: Scholastic Hardcover, 1993), 4.

12. Evans, Joan, *Magical Jewels of the Middle Ages and the Renaissance* (New York: Dover Publications, 1976), 18.

6. Daring to Live Authentically

1. Cynthia Voigt, *David and Jonathan* (New York: Scholastic Hardcover, 1992), 46.

2. Edna Edwards, *ALAN Review*, Spring 1992, 24; Roger Sutton, *Bulletin of the Center for Children's Books*, April 1992, 223.

3. Marcus Crouch, *The School Librarian*, August 1992, 115.

4. Cathi MacRae, *Wilson Library Bulletin*, May 1992, 131; Peter Hollindale, *Times Educational Supplement*, 3 April 1992, 33.

5. Hazel Rochman, *Booklist*, 1 March 1992, 1270; hereafter cited in the text.

6. Cynthia Voigt, *Glass Mountain* (New York: Harcourt, Brace, Jovanovich, 1991), 1.

7. Donald Barthelme, *City Life* (New York: Farrar, Straus, and Giroux, 1970), 65.

8. Saul Bellow, epigraph to *Glass Mountain*.

9. Cynthia Ogorek, *Booklist*, 1 November 1991, 495.

10. Shirley Fetherwolf, *The Book Report*, May 1992, 47.

11. Douglas Glover, *Book World*, 29 December 1991, 9.

12. *Publisher's Weekly*, 9 August 1991, 44.

13. Arlene Bathgate, *School Library Journal*, April 1922, 164.

14. Cynthia Voigt, *Seventeen Against the Dealer* (New York: Ballantine Books, 1989), 17–18.

15. Diane Roback, *Publisher's Weekly*, 14 September 1992, 125; hereafter cited in the text.

16. Cynthia Voigt, *Orfe* (New York: Atheneum, 1992), 8.

17. Jacob Grimm and Wilhelm Grimm, *Grimms' Fairy Tales*, trans. E. V. Lucas, Lucy Crane, and Marian Edwardes (New York: Grosset & Dunlap, 1945), 190.

18. Bruno Bettelheim, *The Uses of Enchantment: The Meaning and Importance of Fairy Tales* (New York: Knopf, 1976), 289; hereafter cited in the text.

19. Stevie Smith, *The Frog Prince and Other Poems* (New York: Longmans, 1966), 88.

20. Interview with Cati Coulthard, December 1992.

21. Cynthia Voigt, *When She Hollers* (New York: Scholastic Hardcover, 1994), 30.

7. Voigt's Essential Ideas: A Thematic Overview

1. Ginette Castro, *American Feminism: A Contemporary History* (New York: New York University Press, 1990), 239; hereafter cited in the text.

2. Denise Wilms and Irene Cooper, eds., *A Guide to Non-Sexist Children's Books: 1976–1985*, vol. 2 (Chicago: Academy Chicago Publishers, 1987), ix.

3. Naomi Wolf, *The Beauty Myth* (New York: William Morrow, 1991), 60.

4. Don McAdams, *Power, Intimacy, and the Life Story* (New York: Guilford, 1988), 42.

5. J. Rohrlich, *Work and Love* (New York: Summit Books, 1980).

6. Ann Douglas, *The Feminization of American Culture* (New York: Knopf, 1977), 52.

7. Joseph Campbell, *The Hero with a Thousand Faces* (Princeton: Princeton University Press, 1986), 337.

Selected Bibliography

Primary Works

Novels

Building Blocks. New York: Atheneum, 1984.
The Callender Papers. New York: Atheneum, 1983.
Come a Stranger. New York: Atheneum, 1986.
David and Jonathan. New York: Atheneum, 1991.
Dicey's Song. New York: Atheneum, 1983.
Glass Mountain. New York: Harcourt, Brace, Jovanovich, 1992.
Homecoming. New York: Atheneum, 1981.
Izzy, Willy-Nilly. New York: Atheneum, 1986.
Jackaroo. New York: Ballantine Books, 1985.
On Fortune's Wheel. New York: Ballantine Books, 1990.
Orfe. New York: Atheneum, 1992.
The Runner. New York: Atheneum, 1985.
Seventeen Against the Dealer. New York: Ballantine Books, 1989.
A Solitary Blue. New York: Atheneum, 1983
Sons from Afar. New York: Atheneum, 1987.
Tell Me If the Lovers Are Losers. New York: Atheneum, 1982.
Tree by Leaf. New York: Ballantine Books, 1988.
The Vandemark Mummy. New York: Ballantine Books, 1991.
When She Hollers. New York: Scholastic, 1994.
The Wings of a Falcon. New York: Scholastic, 1993.

Children's Books

Stories About Rosie. Illustrated by Dennis Kendrick. New York: Atheneum, 1986.

Speech

Newbery Acceptance Speech. *Horn Book*, August 1983, 401.

Secondary Works

Books and Parts of Books

Beetz, K., and S. Niemeyer, eds. *Beacham's Guide to Literature for Young Adults*. New York: Beacham, 1989.

Butler, Francelia, and Richard Rotert. *Triumphs of the Spirit in Children's Literature*. New York: Library Professional Publications, 1986.

Commire, Anne, ed. *Something About the Author*. Detroit: Gale Research, 1987.

Donelson, Kenneth L., and Aileen Pace Nilsen. *Literature for Today's Young Adults*. Glenview, Ill.: Scott, Foresman, 1989.

Gallo, Don. *Speaking for Ourselves*. Urbana, Ill.: National Council of Teachers of English, 1990.

Gillespie, John, ed. *Best Books for Junior High Readers*. New Providence, N.J.: R. R. Bowker, 1990.

Gillespie, John, ed. *Best Books for Senior High Readers*. New Providence, N.J.: R. R. Bowker, 1991.

Jameson, Gloria. "The Triumphs of the Spirit in Cynthia Voigt's Homecoming, Dicey's Song, *and* A Solitary Blue.*" In* Triumphs of the Spirit in Children's Literature. *Ed. Francelia Butler and Richard Rotert. New York: Library Professional Publications, 1986.*

Lukens, Rebecca J., ed. A Critical Handbook of Children's Literature. *3d. ed. Glenview, Ill.: Scott, Foresman, 1986.*

Metzger, L., and D. Straub, eds. Contemporary Authors: New Revision Series. *Detroit: Gale Research, 1986.*

Moynihan, William, and Mary Shaner, eds. Masterworks of Children's Literature. *New York: Stonehill, 1986.*

Robertson, Debra. Portraying Persons with Disabilities: An Annotated Bibliography of Fiction for Children and Teenagers. *New Providence, N.J.: R. R. Bowker, 1992.*

Senick, Gerald J., and Melissa Reiff Hug, eds. "Cynthia Voigt." In Children's Literature Review. *Detroit: Gale Research, 1987.*

Articles

Dresang, Eliza T. "A Newbery Song for Gifted Readers." *School Library Journal*, 3 November 1983, 33–37.

Henke, James. "Dicey, Odysseus, and Hansel and Gretel: The Lost Children in Voigt's *Homecoming*." *Children's Literature in Education*, Spring 1985, 45–52.

Hoffman, Mary. "Growing Up: A Survey." *Children's Literature in Education*, Winter 1984, 171–85.

Plotz, Judith. "The Disappearance of Childhood: Parent-Child Role Reversals in *After the First Death* and *A Solitary Blue.*" *Children's Literature in Education*, 1988, 2.

Shadiow, Linda. "Recommended: Cynthia Voigt." *English Journal*, April 1987, 71.

Shaw-Eagle, Joanna. "Cynthia Voigt: Family Comes First." *The Christian Science Monitor*, 13 May 1983, B2.

Interviews

Bennett, David. "Authorgraph No. 66: Cynthia Voigt." *Books For Keeps*, 1 Januray 1991, 12–13.

Kauffman, Dorothy. "Profile: Cynthia Voigt." *Language Arts*, December 1985, 876–80.

Voigt, Cynthia. "Writing of *A Solitary Blue.*" *Language Arts*, November 1983, 1026.

Selected Book Reviews

Building Blocks
Burns, Mary. *Hornbook*, August 1984, 470–71.
Cooper, Ilene. *Booklist*, 15 May 1984, 1350.
Sachs, Elizabeth. *New Directions for Women*, Spring 1986, 13.

The Callender Papers
Heins, Ethel. *Hornbook*, August 1983, 458.
Kirkus Reviews, 15 March 1983, 308.
McKinley, Robin. *Children's Book Review Service*, Spring 1983, 128.
Publishers Weekly, 11 March 1983, 86–87.
Slung, Michelle. "Adolescent Heroes," *Booklist*, 8 May 1983, 14.

Come a Stranger
Behrman, Christine. *School Library Journal*, 2 October 1986, 184.
Bradburn, Frances. *Wilson Library Bulletin*, January 1987, 61.
Sutton, Roger. *Bulletin of the Center for Children's Books*, October 1986, 40.
Twichell, Ethel. *The Horn Book Magazine*, November 1986, 749.

David and Jonathan
Crouch, Marcus. *The School Librarian*, August 1992, 115.
Edwards, Edna. *ALAN Review*, Spring 1992, 22.
Hollindale, Peter. *Times Educational Supplement*, 3 April 1992, 33.
MacRae, Cathi. *Wilson Library Bulletin*, May 1992, 107.
Rochman, H. *Booklist*, 1 March 1992, 1270.

Dicey's Song
Barham, Carole. *Voice Youth Advocates*, April 1983, 42.

Fader, Ellen. *School Library Journal*, January 1983, 89.

Hammond, Nancy. *Horn Book*, December 1982, 653–54.

Salway, Lance. "Fiction: *Dicey's Song.*" *The Signal Selection of Children's Books 1984*, New York: Thimble Press, 1985, 20.

Sutherland, Zena. *Bulletin of the Center for Children's Books*, October 1982, 38.

Wilms, Denise. *Booklist*, 1 September 1982, 49–50.

Glass Mountain

Anderson, Dawn. *Library Journal*, 15 October, 124.

Bathgate, Arlene. *School Library Journal*, April 1992, 164.

Fetherwolf, Shirley. *Book Report*, May 1992, 47.

Glover, Douglas. *Book World*, 29 December 1991, 9.

Ogorek, Cynthia. *Booklist*, 1 November 1991, 495.

Publisher's Weekly, 9 August 1991, 44.

Homecoming

Colwell, Elizabeth. *The Junior Bookshelf*, 3 June 1984, 147.

Kaye, Marilyn. *School Library Journal*, April 1981, 144.

Klockner, Karen. *The Horn Book Magazine*, August 1981, 438–39.

Leverich, Kathleen. *New York Times Book Review*, 10 May 1981, 38.

Stein, Ruth. *Language Arts*, 1 January 1982, 55–56.

Izzy, Willy-Nilly

Bulletin of the Center for Children's Books, May 1986, 179.

Burket, Mary Lou. *Book World*, 11 May 1986, 17.

Campbell, Patty. *Wilson Library Bulletin*, November 1986, 49.

Cummins, Julie. *School Library Journal*, April 1986, 101.

Nelms, Ben, and Beth Nelms. *English Journal*, April 1987, 83.

Publishers Weekly, 25 April 1986, 79.

Thomson, Pat. *Books for Keeps*, July 1992, 26.

Jackaroo

Burns, Mary. *Horn Book*, March 1986, 210.

Campbell, Patty. *Wilson Library Bulletin*, March 1986, 50–51.

Clark, Hattie. "Adventures of a Spunky Medieval Heroine," *The Christian Science Monitor*, 1 November 1985, B1.

Nelms, Ben, and Beth Nelms. *English Journal*, February 1986, 106.

Publishers Weekly, 9 August 1985, 77.

Smith, Karen. *School Library Journal*, December 1985, 96.

On Fortune's Wheel

Belden, Elizabeth, and Judith Beckman. *English Journal*, January 1991, 79.

Flowers, Ann. *Horn Book*, May 1990, 341.

Hepler, Susan. *School Library Journal*, March 1990, 242.

Publisher's Weekly, 16 March 1990, 70.

Rochman, Hazel. *Booklist*, 15 February 1990, 1156.

Watson, Victor. *Times Educational Supplement*, 17 May 1991, 28.

Orfe

Fader, Ellen. *Horn Book*, November 1992, 731.

Publisher's Weekly, 14 September, 1992, 125.

Roback, Diane. *Publisher's Weekly*, 14 September 1992, 125.

Sacks, David. *New York Times Book Review*, 8 November 1992, 48.

The Runner

Chumbley-Lora, Alice. *English Journal*, April 1988, 83.

Crouch, M. *The Junior Bookshelf*, June 1986, 119–20.

Digilio, Alice. *Book World*, 14 July 1985, 8.

Goodin, Kathleen. *Interracial Books for Children Bulletin*, 1985, 16.

Hoffman, Mary. *Times Educational Supplement*, 25 April 1986, 28.

Lynn, Ruth Nadelman. *Horn Book*, May 1985, 321–22.

Nelms, Beth, Ben Nelms, and Linda Horton. *English Journal*, September 1985, 84.

Publishers Weekly, 26 August 1985, 82.

Rochman, Hazel. *Booklist*, 15 March 1985, 1052.

Seventeen Against the Dealer

Chu, Nancy. *Booktalker*, November 1989, 12.

Jones, Trev. *School Library Journal*, February 1989, 103.

Ley, Terry. *English Journal*, March 1991, 85.

Rochman, Hazel. *Booklist*, 15 March 1989, 1276.

A Solitary Blue

Flanagan, Kate. *Horn Book*, October 1983, 587.

Jobe, Ronald. *Language Arts*, November 1983, 1025–26.

Kirkus Reviews, 1 September 1983, 1178–79.

Langton, Jane. *New York Times Book Review*, 27 November 1983, 34.

Martin-Leff, Ann. *New Directions for Women*, May 1985, 20.

Rohmann, Gloria. *School Library Journal*, September 1983, 139–40.

Sons from Afar

Bradburn, Frances. *Wilson Library Journal*, April 1988, 72.

Books for Keeps, July 1989, 13.

Ley, Terry. *English Journal*, November 1989, 81.

Publishers Weekly, 14 August 1987, 106.

Wilms, Denise. *Booklist*, 15 September 1987, 154.

Zeiger, Hanna. *Horn Book*, March 1988, 214.

Tell Me If the Lovers Are Losers

Bulletin of the Center for Children's Books, April 1982, 159.

Estes, Sally. *Booklist*, 15 March 1982, 950.

McKenzie, Joe. *School Library Journal*, 28 May 1982, 88.

Rosser, Claire. *Kliatt Young Adult Paperback Book Guide*, 17 September 1983, 20.

Tree by Leaf

Bradburn, Frances. *Wilson Library Bulletin*, June 1988, 110.

Bulletin of the Center for Children's Books, April 1988, 171.

Leimbach, Dulcie. *New York Times Book Review*, 12 June 1988, 35.

Ley, Terry. *English Journal*, March 1990, 80.

Publisher's Weekly, 26 February 1988, 198.

Sawyer, Kem. *Book World*, 10 April 1988, 12.

Watson, Elizabeth S. *Hornbook*, June 1988, 363.

Wilms, Denise. *Booklist*, 1 April 1988, 1355.

The Vandemark Mummy

Brewbaker, Jim. *ALAN Review*, Fall 1992, 22.

Cooper, Ilene. *Booklist*, 1 September 1991, 46.

Kirkus Reviews, 15 September 1991, 1229.

Publisher's Weekly, 9 August 1991, 58.

Watson, Elizabeth. *Horn Book*, November 1991, 739.

Stories About Rosie

Brachman, Kathleen. *School Library Journal*, October 1986, 167.

Hearne, Betsy. *Bulletin of the Center for Children's Books*, December 1986, 78.

Publishers Weekly, 26 September 1986, 82.

Index

The Author

Suzanne Reid has taught English and English Education at Radford University, Emory & Henry College, and Virginia Highlands Community College in southwest Virginia. She is the author of articles about young adult literature in the *ALAN Review* and *Signal,* and also writes about collaborative educational research in the *Virginia English Bulletin* and in the *Yearbook for the National Reading Association.* At present, she lives in Emory, Virginia with her husband, Robin, and her two children, Jenny and Tristan.

The Editor

Patricia J. Campbell is an author and critic specializing in books for young adults. She has taught adolescent literature at the University of California, Los Angeles, and she is the former Assistant Coordinator of Young Adult Services for the Los Angeles Public Library. Her literary criticism has been published in the *New York Times Book Review* and many other journals. From 1978 to 1988 her column "The YA Perplex," a monthly review of young adult books, appeared in the *Wilson Library Bulletin*. She now writes a review column on the independent press for that magazine, and a column on controversial issues in adolescent literature for *Horn Book* magazine. Campbell is the author of five books, among them *Presenting Robert Cormier*, the first volume in the Twayne Young Adult Author Series. In 1989 she was the recipient of the American Library Association Grolier Award for distinguished achievement with young people and books. A native of Los Angeles, Campbell now lives on an avocado ranch near San Diego, where she and her husband, David Shore, write and publish books on overseas motor-home travel.